LE**A**DING MATTERS

LE**A**DING MATTERS

An Inspirational and Practical Approach
for High-Performance Leaders

MICHAEL   DEBORAH
MORIN   DICKSON

GSPH

GENERAL STORE PUBLISHING HOUSE
499 O'Brien Road, Box 415
Renfrew, Ontario, Canada K7V 4A6
Telephone 1.613.432.7697 or 1.800.465.6072
www.gsph.com

ISBN 978-1-897508-88-6

Cover art, design, formatting: Magdalene Carson / New Leaf Publication Design
Printed by Custom Printers of Renfrew Ltd., Renfrew, Ontario
Printed and bound in Canada

Library and Archives Canada Cataloguing in Publication

Morin, Michael, 1944-

Leading matters : an inspirational and practical handbook for

leaders / Michael Morin, Deborah Dickson.

ISBN 978-1-897508-88-6

1. Leadership. I. Dickson, Deborah, 1952- II. Title.

HM1261.M66 2010 303.3'4 C2010-904104-6

Dedicated to:

Cheryl Morin and Dave Dickson

*for understanding that
we needed to do this*

and to:

Rob Notman

President and CEO, KWA Partners (Ottawa) Limited

Jim Sevigny

Vice-president and General Manager, KWA Partners (Ottawa) Limited

Margot Sevigny

Executive Vice-president, KWA Partners (Ottawa) Limited

for making sure we did.

*Our thanks also go to the many who helped,
abetted, and encouraged us:*

▶ *Our Leadership Interviewees — for their incredible
insights and contributions*

▶ *KWA Partners (Ottawa) Limited management and
staff — for continual support and encouragement (and
Donna Eden's critical eye)*

▶ *Our Coalition Team — our sounding board:*
Brent A. Fehr, Vice President, Front Street Capital
Stephen Bent, Branch Manager, CIBC
*Norman Hotchkiss, Managing Director, Hotchkiss
International*
*Dave Boshard, P. Eng., Vice President Business
Development, Gridway Computing Corporation*
Marion Barfurth, Ph.D.
*Stephen Heckbert, Professor and Coordinator, Public
Relations Program, Algonquin College*

Dany Levasseur, Regional Director, Brookfield LePage, Johnston Controls

Andrée Mongeon, Senior Communications Advisor, Canadian Nuclear Safety Commission

Michele Langlois, Senior Consultant, BP&M Consulting

Denise Belanger, Associate Director, University of Ottawa Health Services – Family Health Team

Colleen Ryan, Consultant, Learning Design, Development and Project Management

Theresa Howe, Senior Marketing Strategist, McMillan

Fatima Robertson, CMA, MBA

Gary Herman, Colonel, United States Air Force, Retired

▶ *Dave Dickson, Managing Partner (retired), KPMG, Ottawa – for clarity*

▶ *Joseph Morin, Associate Editor,* Kemptville Advance, *Metroland Media, Ottawa Region – our editorial and creative guide*

▶ *Tim Gilmor, Ph.D. – for encouragement*

▶ *David Atkinson, President, Kwantlen Polytechnic University – for encouragement*

▶ *Roch Brisson, Vice President, Finance, Minto Corporation – for providing a place to write*

▶ *Dr. Pamela Eisener-Parsche, Chief of Staff, Bruyère Continuing Care – for having confidence in us*

▶ *Career and Leadership Clients of KWA Partners – for your enthusiasm and support.*

▶ *General Store Publishing House*

Tim Gordon, publisher – for his professional enthusiasm and support

Jane Karchmar – for her editing and unflagging patience

Magdalene Carson – for her boundless creativity and beautiful designs

Contents

Preface

"In these tough times, it can't be about popularity or
'pop' fixes; it must be about intentional and consistent
leadership and good decisions based upon what we
know works, from the experiences of our past."

Michael and Deborah, 2009

We thought we knew something about leadership. We talked about it. We read about it. We even led, from time to time.

"The more we thought we knew, the more we realized that we needed to know what we didn't know."

If you are trying to learn something about something you don't know, and you have tried the traditional talking, reading, and practising methods, all that is left is to ask those who have proven they already know – those who have proven themselves (widely or privately) – to help fill the gaps. And so, we asked. What we were given were insights into leadership from an applied perspective.

This applied leadership approach to twenty-first-century challenges, using tried and true leadership techniques, flows from interviews with local leaders filtered by our understanding and experience.

Why leadership? Why now?

The circumstances we find ourselves in now – financial collapse, recession, and recovery, technology boom and bust and boom again, failure of the "anointed leaders" to live up to fundamental character and value codes—have created twenty-first-century workplace turbulence that has caught us unprepared. These new and unsettling circumstances have created more career and employment uncertainty than North America, or the world, for that matter, has experienced since the "Dirty Thirties."

At the same time, the demands on business leaders to keep up with the rate of change and turbulence and to be positioned to take advantage of the recovery momentum has created an insatiable appetite for even more creative management processes, a more highly skilled workforce, and a longer-term yet agile vision in order to just survive, let alone prosper.

On the one hand, we have enormous workplace turbulence, information overload, and change growth that often obscure our ability to see the future. This change rate has been accompanied by increasingly complex management and human resource challenges. On the other side of things, we see an extraordinarily talented Canadian workforce waiting for leaders to lead. Leaders are needed to step up and start applying direct and intentional influence to align value with vision and with people, bringing the hope of individual and team maximum value to the challenges we face.

Why you?

Rather than waiting for someone else to step up, you have the power and permission to step up for yourself and others. In order to help you, we have assembled the information in this book, accumulated leadership knowledge garnered from the School of Hard Knocks. Normally you learn these lessons by experiencing the successes and failures in your own career and life. You continue to learn, but our research has produced a shortcut to proven leadership ideas that will help you better appreciate what works and what won't. More important, we provide you with easy-to-understand leadership priorities and tools that will help you get the best from yourself and from those you choose to influence (alternatively, from those who have given you permission to lead).

Why us?

At times in our lives, we find ourselves in positions of influence – places where we can make a difference. This is where we find ourselves now. We have experienced the highs and lows that positive leadership or a leadership vacuum can bring. We have been leaders and followers. We have experienced success and failure in the public, private, and entrepreneurial sectors. We are neither spring chickens nor are we "Polly Annas" – although it might sound trite to say we have been there and done that.

Inspired by a shared passion for practical leadership, a shared interest in seeing others be the best they can be, and a serendipitous relationship with a caring and forward-thinking organization, we have been able to bring our minds together for the development and delivery of this approach. Our intention is to help you in all your relationships – in your work, your family, your community, and within yourself – to achieve maximum performance based on your values and vision.

Introduction

L eadership affects quality of life, culture, and just about every sector of a society.

Genuine leadership abilities are often a mystery. Leading by force and leading by chance are no substitutes for leading with character and intellect.

The twenty-first century has many examples of failed leadership, leaving in their wake worldwide economic and social chaos, the effects of which are felt from a Mom and Pop store in any neighbourhood to the head office of some of the most prestigious and successful global corporations.

Seeking out good leadership in its many forms is the first step in finding it.

It is no surprise that the path to a better understanding of what leadership is and why leadership matters began with a conversation between two people whose job it was to help rebuild confidence and purpose in those who had been affected by a lack of leadership.

"Michael and I met in the summer of 2006," remembers Deborah. "I was a transition client of KWA Partners, moving from an executive leadership role in a large corporation. Michael was the senior transition coach at KWA Partners assisting with the development of search plans and materials."

Michael's and Deborah's conversations seemed to naturally evolve into questions about the importance of leadership and how leadership can fail organizations and individuals.

Michael recalled, "I had seen hundreds of clients before Deborah and, although I had heard from them a similar curiosity about the role leadership played in their transition – good, bad, and indifferent – it wasn't until our conversations that it struck me."

There seemed to be two factors at play.

The first factor was that the majority of people Michael was working with were good people with good skills.

The second factor was that they had all wanted to be successful and were all looking for the chance to follow a good leader.

Deborah says, "We talked at length about leadership and its impact on individuals and organizations."

Deborah felt that their conversations and conclusions were important enough to share with other clients and acquaintances. "Increasingly," she says, "We found a ravenous appetite for the discussion of practical, applied leadership ideas that could be used to guide people into a higher level of performance and into organizations that fit their values. It quickly became apparent, however, that apart from our mutually intuitive and somewhat superficial leadership ideas, we had a lot of passion but not much content to pass on to others."

Michael was already doing some work delivering some broad leadership concepts through the KWA Partners (Ottawa) Limited client seminars, but the material he was using was based on feelings and intuition. If a way were to be found to focus the delivery of the leadership concept, he had to first acquire a broad range of practical leadership ideas – that really worked – from leaders that had a proven track record of high leadership performance.

"I don't know where it came from," he explains, "but the idea emerged to simply interview people whom we viewed as exceptional leaders."

Deborah's response was enthusiastic. "What a wonderful and insightful plan – using the wealth of talent in our backyard to serve as the inspiration for our leadership tips."

The next step was identifying who would contribute their leadership experiences to Michael and Deborah. "At this point," says Deborah," we were ready to do it regardless – with or without assistance; we just had to do it."

With support from KWA Partners (Ottawa) Limited and urging from former clients who perceived a lack of leadership in the modern world, Michael and Deborah set out to develop their plan.

Michael says, "Around the same time, a lunchroom encounter with Jim Sevigny, the VP for Business Development at KWA Partners (Ottawa) Limited, resulted in the idea to develop the basic leadership seminar I had been delivering to transition clients into a more comprehensive set of leadership tools and products. Talk about timing!

"Normally when I am in the midst of a significant decision (personal or business), I like to bounce my ideas off of trusted friends and colleagues. These are people who I know will give me the straight goods. In this case, I invited Norm Hotchkiss (a former transition client) and five others (Gary Herman, a U.S. Air Force retired colonel, and other former clients Dany Levasseur, Brent Fehr, Stephen Bent, and Dave Boshard) to give me advice on what we were thinking about doing. Their unanimous support and enthusiasm sealed the deal. We were about to launch the 'Leadership in the Workplace' project."

Deborah adds, "With Michael's Leadership Coalition commitment behind us and with Jim's 'can you' question in front of us, we developed a business plan and proposal and delivered it to the executive team at KWA Partners (Ottawa) Limited."

With everyone on the same page, the task of collecting what eventually became "nuggets of wisdom" was undertaken.

The result is *Leading Matters* — a book with a clear sense of what leadership is and how to learn to exercise it, excel in it, and share it.

THE WALL

Jacquelin Holzman	Jean Boyle	Jan Kaminski	Jean-Pierre Soubliere	Rob Lindsay
Jim Orban	Roger Greenberg	Franklin Holtforster	Gerry Arial	Jim Durrell
France Jacovela	John Watts	Rosemarie Leclair	Shannon Tessler	Dave Dickson
Brent Fehr	Andrée Mongeon	Stephen Bent	Colleen Ryan	David Boshard
Denise Belanger	Marion Barfurth	Norm Hotchkiss	Theresa Howe	Stephen Heckbert
Gary Herman	Dany Levasseur	Joe Morin	Fatima Robertson	Michele Langlois
Donna Eden	Tammy Hoffman	Doug Tansley	Josée Robillard	Pauline O'Leary
Lyn Densmore	David Atkinson	Tim Gilmor	Charles Vallerand	James Reid	Marcy Comeau
Colene O'Brien	Rob Notman	Michael Morin	Deborah Dickson	Jim Sevigny	Margot Sevigny

Our "wall" of support was built one idea at a time and one helpful thought or act at a time. To those who helped us, we are truly grateful. In Section 5 you will find the biographies of the interesting people whom we interviewed.

Throughout the book, we have embedded the nuggets and ideas from our research to connect practical and applied leadership ideas to the challenges we all face in these ever-changing times. What follows is what we have taken from these interviews and nuggets and how we think they will be useful to you. We have tried to present a logical progression of observations and ideas, as we see them.

It is inevitable that in presentation we had to create a theoretical framework to hold all the ideas and materials to make them logical and readable — but make no mistake: Applied leadership is not about theory, it is about the passionate use of influence to create great and positive outcomes.

SECTION ONE

The Challenge

How many good leaders do you know? How many people would you follow with confidence and trust, especially in these times? Do you belong to a team that understands where they are headed and why? Does your team behave with a set of values that is consistent with yours?

Values that guarantee you never have to compromise on the fundamental principles of doing the right things for the right reasons in the right way? If so, congratulations! Savour and enjoy the successes that will come your team's way. If you are not on such a team (and you will know if you are not), we will try to provide some context to what is going on.

First things first.

Every leader that we interviewed – and in fact every leader we have come across in our daily lives – has a philosophy by which he/she tries to live. The most successful of these share a life philosophy based on helping others. We are not saying that the leaders we know are trying to be nominated for sainthood, but they are truly interested in helping to make others better. In fact, Jacquelin Holzman reinforced this view in our interview with her, as expressed in the first nugget on the following page.

When we looked a little deeper, we found that leaders using this notion of helping were looking to develop high-performance teams, with high-performance results for everyone, including themselves.

I wanted to always leave things better off than when I found them in the first place (Leadership Ottawa is an example).

Jacquelin Holzman

A leader is entitled to lead to the extent that people are willing to follow. Leadership is the measure of the extent to which you can compel others *to choose* to follow.

Franklin Holtforster

Make sure you are trying to make things better. Even when you think you are, check and make sure again.

Michael Morin

Followers all want to grow and develop. That doesn't mean that they all want to be the leader or displace the CEO. They just may want to keep learning, moving forward, growing, following the vision.

Shannon Tessier

LEADERSHIP FUNDAMENTALS

The Leader's Philosophy:
How can I help you?

How All Leaders Project:
Enthusiastically, Openly,
Optimistically, Forthrightly

The Best Leaders are also:
Honest, Ethical

How Leaders Succeed:
- ▶ Self Knowledge/Authenticity
- ▶ Leadership Value Proposition
- ▶ Vision and Values
- ▶ Coaching others/Collaboration
- ▶ Building Trust
- ▶ Credibility/Authority

These leaders were identified by their followers as being worthy of leading and were given permission to lead. They tended to be enthusiastic, perhaps even passionate. They are definitely open, optimistic, and forthright. What we found was that when the leader projected this kind of image, the followers tended to accept on faith that the leader could not only lead but would lead honestly and ethically.

The kinds of leaders we are talking about are those who practise these characteristics consistently, aiming to leave things better than when they found them.

Of course, there are always some who appear to represent these characteristics but their intention is to only better themselves, perhaps at the expense of others. Trust us when we say that these are not leaders to be followed. History is replete with famous examples of these types of pretenders and the damage they can cause. They do have a following, but not here.

Our interest is in helping those who wish to lead and exert influence for the most positive of reasons. More about that later.

I think that the final measure of our real potential as leaders will be our willingness to reach out, to explore, to push the boundaries, and to grow and learn. In this century this is essential and it's also very cool.

Shannon Tessier

— — — — — — — — — — — — — — — — —

You can't be a leader today and not a leader tomorrow. You are always a leader. That's who you are. You don't arrive here and put your leader hat on.

France Jacovella

— — — — — — — — — — — — — — —

I know that there are huge areas of business that I don't understand; I rely on the ones I trust, who have the expertise to fill my knowledge gaps. I recognize my limitations and I won't pretend to know things that I don't. If I try to cram more information into my head than can fit, something else has to suffer. I prefer to just ask others to help. Now, that doesn't mean that I won't test those whose expertise I ask for; I certainly will. But I can't — I won't — try to do it all myself.

Roger Greenberg

How do leaders succeed? Our conclusion is that leaders who work hard to master at least six core themes have the best chance to build high-performance teams.

The six themes are:

- ▶ Self-Knowledge and Authenticity
- ▶ Leadership Value Proposition
- ▶ Vision and Values
- ▶ Coaching Others and Collaboration
- ▶ Building Trust
- ▶ Credibility and Authority

Each of these themes is presented and discussed later in Section 3, along with self-assessment tools that will help *you* to see where *you* stand in each area. There are of course other leadership competency issues and concepts, but in the end, these six seem to give a leader the best possible chance of attaining the highest level of performance. All our leader interviewees backed up this perspective.

Three key factors

At any stage in your career and life there are three factors that you bring to the table: education; skill/experience; and your maximum value proposition. These are the three basic components that present a complete version of you.

> **WHAT YOU BRING TO THE TABLE:**
> Education
> Skill and Experience
> Your Maximum Value Proposition

Education is the start. Throughout our lives we are always learning – sometimes formally, sometimes informally. The education that you achieve at any given point defines a new start line – a new level of credibility. Every leader we spoke to indicated that continuous learning is a key component of skilful and successful leading. We were not surprised.

People can see, by the look in your eyes and by your actions, if you are authentic or not — and if you are trying to lead them when or where they don't want to be led. If you are straight-up, sort of "here it is," in good times or bad, your leadership abilities will remain untarnished and you will stay authentic.

Jim Durrell

I am convinced that your leadership potential is first shaped by your family and parents long before your work starts influencing your leadership reality.

Rob Lindsay

Somewhere in the character of the people we hire, they want to be project leaders and in the project environment, if not corporate leaders. They want to know that they will be equipped for that leadership role. That matters to a large portion of them. We call this maximum value.

Franklin Holtforster

The first task of leaders is to spend time and make the effort to look inside themselves, to find their values and strengths, and to come to understand their authentic selves.

Jim Durrell

I probably admire people who lead and who also know how to follow. "Follower-ship" is one of the things that I really admire. Strong leaders really understand when their role is to lead and when their role is to follow.

Jan Kaminski

Just as knowledge creates a new opportunity to rise to higher levels, absence of knowledge can eliminate or cripple leadership opportunities. That is not to say that leaders need to know everything about everything, but they have to know what they don't know. We are not talking about modesty in this level of understanding. The intention is not to underestimate what you know but rather to truly understand strengths and undeveloped areas so that you can build the right kind of supporting team around yourself. We have provided some exercises in Section 3 to help you come to know what you know and don't know.

The second factor is our expression of skill reflected in experience. We do not see experience as a passive view of the past, but as proof that we've "been there, done that, got the T-shirt." Understanding how our experiences have influenced us is a key component of authenticity that our followers need to clearly see.

These two aspects are fact-based and are fairly easy to examine, record, and draw lessons from. This is a major part of your "career" resume. Your "leadership" resume includes much more.

Your Maximum Value Proposition

The "much more" we are talking about is your "Maximum Value Proposition" (MVP). Simply put, your MVP is the 20 percent that produces your 80 percent.[1] Understanding what it is for you and behaving toward others in alignment with it sends a message to others about your true leadership value.

This would be the authentic *you*. As we interact, we are always exerting influence. The value of our MVP determines the willingness of others to be influenced. If others assign to you a high MVP because of what they see in you, what they hear from you, and what their interactions with you lead to, then they are likely to be open to your influence and will be predisposed to follow.

It is not enough to simply be seen as having a high MVP, but it is a beginning. It allows a foundation for the rest of the leadership value that you create and use. Make no mistake: this is a hard path to follow. Once your MVP is established in others' perception, departures from this proposition are generally

1   Richard Koch, *The 80/20 Individual* (New York: Doubleday, 2003).

The ability of the person and his/her desire to perform will always trump process, so you'd better have the person believing in the right things.

Roger Greenberg

— — — — — — — — — — — — — — — — — —

My intuition about people and things is a huge factor in my leadership style. Your intuitive capacity must be drawn from your exposure to difficult circumstances, not just the good times. You need to have won and lost and still want to lead; that's when you are learning. If the passion is not there, you fade away, perhaps thinking that leading wasn't as much fun as you thought it would be.

Jim Durrell

— — — — — — — — — — — — — — — — —

I won't work with those who are not interested in learning, in changing, in reaching some form of their maximum value. I'll even take those whom I clearly can't keep in my business, who will most certainly leave for their own visions, their own greener pastures. We're all better off for the effort I make to teach and they to learn.

Gerry Arial

— — — — — — — — — — — — — — — — —

Some people will learn leadership techniques by study, by attending retreats, and so on, but *everyone* learns by doing.

J-P Soublière

— — — — — — — — — — — — — — — — —

When you are leading, expect that a lot of what will happen to you will not be nice, might be unfair, and might hurt. Things said against you might not be true. Your self-image and confidence have to survive these things, so take care to understand yourself and your strengths.

Jim Durrell

difficult to forgive and might undermine your ability to lead in the future. There have been many who have fallen.

> ## MAXIMUM VALUE PROPOSITION
>
> ### Maximum Value Proposition integrates:
>
> ▶ Personal history and attributes
> ▶ Competitiveness, standards, and confidence
> ▶ Willingness to keep learning while honestly reflecting on past failures and successes
> ▶ Continuous growth *and* understanding leadership skill, knowledge, and function
> ▶ Strategic and tactical agility in turbulent socio-economic times

Put in perspective, the weights that we might assign to each of the three factors — education, skill/experience, and MVP — are not equal. We consider that MVP is by far the most important and dominant factor. In percentage terms, your MVP represents about 80 percent of your leadership-influencing capacity in both casual and formal settings. Education and experience are obviously important but are more significant in considering what we are *not* specifically qualified to do, rather than being an indication of our leadership capacity.

So what?

Every time you enter a room or meet someone, the demonstration of your maximum value proposition, honestly and authentically, affects the willingness of others to accept that you are offering value that lines up with their needs. They will be ready to listen. They are doing just as you are doing — assigning MVP to everyone they are meeting and determining who is worth listening to. Consider this as an initial, intuitive handshake between MVPs. The conclusion drawn on either side will determine the potential of the relationship.

Each of us has an MVP that is uniquely ours based upon our characteristics and factors. Understand yours, whatever it is.

I have always believed that we needed to be at maximum performance at all times, and occasionally we had to ask for extraordinary performance! I'm not sure if we always got there, but we did okay!

J-P Soublière

—————————————————————

Integrity, creativity, initiative, helping others, accountability, and trust are critically important characteristics of leadership. I like to create and to promote creativity. I like to take action and I prefer for those working with me to assume responsibility and take action as well. I enjoy mentoring and helping others.

Deborah Dickson

—————————————————————

I am a big believer in always networking and always learning. I think that is an integral part of leadership. You are not going to be a leader if you are standing in the corner. You have to be approachable to everybody — at every level. You have to be able to network and establish relationships.

John Watts

—————————————————————

If you take on a new challenge and try to change the culture of that workplace, know this: it is not enough to be charming. A leader must build bridges and close gaps. Build relationships, acknowledge the value that others bring to the table, and somehow orient those capabilities to achieving your goals.

Jim Orban

Be true to it and your capacity and potential as a person and as a leader will rarely be misinterpreted.

There is a dark side to the MVP transmission and reception. We have all met people whom we have assessed initially as having a high MVP – especially if we are practising our open and forthright leadership style – and then have been bitterly disappointed to discover that we have been completely fooled. Their true nature became evident to us through their bad behaviour and poor choices.

We can forgive errors in judgment from others as they attempt to do the right things and get it wrong. But it is much more difficult when we see behaviour that is a clear violation of the value that we assigned in the first place. Sometimes, the violation is unforgivable.

Why is our understanding of ourselves vis-à-vis all three factors so important? Without the confidence that we achieve when we understand ourselves and behave consistently as authentic persons, we will be found out. We will be incapable of influencing in the three critical relationship areas that lead to high performance.

Every leader *at every level* (from the mailroom to the boardroom) is trying to exert the right kind of influence in four dimensions: your leader, your peers, your team, and yourself. Everyone is a leader in some way. No one gets off the hook. Everyone must be accountable.

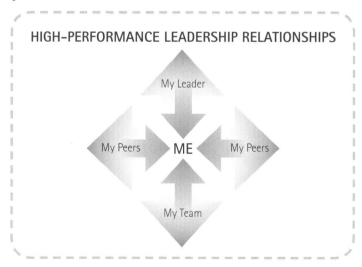

HIGH–PERFORMANCE LEADERSHIP RELATIONSHIPS

My Leader

My Peers   ME   My Peers

My Team

A leader must continually build relationships. This is the most imperative of tasks, especially when the pressure of the moment can consume them. A leader should default to building relationships rather than consuming them. In every conversation, in every interaction, a leader must build up the relationship so that there is something left in the pot when you need it.

Franklin Holtforster

Since change is constant, manage your energy. Keep checking the pulse of your staff (even casual conversations). Establish feedback loops. Review programs regularly by networking. Be visible! No private elevators, no towers! But remember, although you need to understand what is going on in the trenches, you cannot be in the trenches all the time.

Jacquelin Holzman

Leadership might not always look like the sure thing, but it is always the right thing. Remember, all of the problems will rise to the top, and it's the leader who must recognize what they are.

J-P Soublière

Stay visible with your workforce. Engage at all levels. Get out to the shop floor — to the active workforce. Be recognizable and approachable. Every job, every task, every person needs to feel connected to the leadership, if you are to achieve ultimate success.

Rosemarie Leclair

Each of these influencing relationships is affected by your MVP and by your grasp of the strategic and tactical priorities you face. Each of these relationships requires a specific agreement to lead or follow, or sometimes both. And all the relationships will succeed when the values, vision, and behaviours of the participants are in alignment.

We see vision, values, and behaviour as mandatory and fundamental elements that allow a leader to be listened to and allow followers the permission to take the right actions at the right times for the right reasons. This provides agreement on the fundamentals for the high-performance team.

Complicating this is the reality that we all have our own unique view of the world based upon our specific education, experience, and MVP combination as well as the "clutter" or distractions of everyday life. These complications are what make the leadership challenge more art form than science certainty.

Leadership — our definition

Perhaps it's time to give you our definition of what we think leadership actually is.

LEADERSHIP — OUR DEFINITION

▶ Leadership is an art and is the direct and intentional application of influence to cause achievement where otherwise it would not occur.

▶ Leadership is always based upon a vision of the future and can only be effective with those who agree to share the same value, behaviour, and character foundation.

There are scores of definitions for leadership, and that in itself creates a problem for those who are trying to gain some level of understanding about what will work. What we have found is that a leader is facing a series of constantly moving targets that make it clear that the most effective style will be one constantly adjusting to the new circumstances or contexts.

We see the art of the leader as being the most critical component of the art and science requirements for leadership.

I like strong leaders who are intelligent, who can articulate clearly and directly a vision to staff, and then provide them the tools to get the right things done. It's like being on board a ship; here's our port, here are the tools to run this ship, and here is the route we need to follow.

Roger Greenberg

Some people say leaders are born. I don't believe that at all. Early in my life, my father gave me goals; he wanted me to understand that I would face adversity and obstacles but that if I took the leadership initiative, I would be successful. The best way to do that is to just grow and lead throughout your life. Eventually, I learned what he meant. You can't wait for it to come to you. You have to reach out and take it.

Jean Boyle

I do "Leadership by Walking Around." My days were pretty unstructured. Days that I had to be structured were days that I didn't feel I was doing as good a job or as effective a job.

Jan Kaminski

You have to believe that people want to do their best. What really works is talking to people and getting to know them. Do not sit in an office and call them in every six months. This never works, even though everyone tried to make it work. Do it on a daily basis.

Dave Dickson

The good leader takes pains to create the time and opportunity to look beyond the current horizon. Sometimes I really "zone out" and my friends and colleagues make a joke out of it, but I have to take time to think, to get ahead of events, so that my team is prepared.

Jim Durrell

A constant need for leadership agility arises as changing circumstances require leaders to make every effort to keep their leadership *directly* connected to their followers, peers, and superiors. *Direct* means face-to-face, in the moment, transmitting MVP, securing agreement, giving permission, and encouraging high performance.

This is the first of several super-critical requirements of leaders in the twenty-first century. Creating or allowing situations that prevent direct interaction will cripple your leadership influence and prevent followers from being the best they can be. Followers need the value you are offering, that you have earned, that you are being paid for. The most direct way of passing this value on is simply through your contact with them. You cannot hide from this responsibility. We often hear the phrase, "Management by Walking Around" (MBWA) to achieve high-performance results, but "Leading by Walking Around" (LBWA) is infinitely more important.

Leaders lead *intentionally*. Every leader we interviewed had intention. They wanted something. High performance did not happen by accident. Each leader had a specific intention – sometimes more than one. Each of them developed a specific set of actions to cause their intentions to be fulfilled. Each of them took specific action to express those intentions and to move things forward. On this point, one of the characteristics of the successful leader is to provide for the followers a translation of the intent. This translation, or reframing, is extremely important because every leader we spoke to did not assume that the followers would see the same things the same way as the leader.

Leaders understand that everyone sees things from a different vantage point, a different context, a different set of experiences. They understand that they have to provide a clear expression of the intent if the listener is to have a chance of understanding, and if the leader is to have the confidence that the action will be undertaken successfully.

Influencing is more powerful than ordering. When a leader influences, the followers buy in. They accept and commit to the task because they understand the context, the intent, and

This is a key activity for me. I need to see where we've been and where we are going before I move to the next plan.

Rob Lindsay

If you want everyone to be thinking outside the box, you'd better explain to them what the box actually is. Provide a vision and examples of what you need. Hire a facilitator to help you rally the ideas. Challenge your team during creativity sessions to outline what they would do to grow the business. Push the issue; put some timelines and consequences on the table.

Jean Boyle

Basically, employees will "hang in" if there is a good and clear understanding of what the organization is trying to do, that there is a clear version of Value and Character that everyone practises and if there is a consistent and compassionate leadership example for all to emulate and aspire to.

Michael Morin

Leaders make those around them and with them better.

John Watts

You have to show confidence in and support your new-hires. You can't just throw them out there. Work with them. Make sure that you promote them where you can. You will start getting positive, unsolicited comments and compliments.

Jim Orban

the implied (or direct) permission that the leader is extending. Influenced followers will be far more likely to continue the task to a higher standard on their own initiative than an ordered subordinate would feel obligated to do.

The foundation of effective leadership influence is a shared *vision* along with shared values, behaviours, and character fundamentals. With this shared agreement in place, the applied leader can generally be certain that every member is pulling in generally the same direction respecting the same value and behaviour model. This allows everyone freedom to operate at his/her highest possible value knowing that permission is granted, latitude to act is understood, and forgiveness for honest errors will be granted.

Every organization we have worked with where these preconditions did not exist or were not discussed or were not obviously shared was usually an organization underperforming, often under a great deal of stress.

LEADERSHIP CREATES . . .

- Maximum value
- Personal power and independence
- Responsibility
- Permission
- Forgiveness
- Succession
- Trust
- Courage
- Motivation

. . . A BETTER RESULT THAN SCIENCE PREDICTED

The future for these organizations is far less bright than it could have been. This idea – that leadership is powerful – is shared by our interviewees.

In addition to the power of MVP, permission, forgiveness, and responsibility, the applied leader is constantly developing others in order to pass success for the team forward. This is not about preparing others to fill our shoes, but rather to "stand them on our shoulders."

I hold nothing back from employees, even when they might be planning to move on and get into business for themselves. This renewal will make us all stronger in the end. Leaders need to be open and encouraging, mentoring as they go. This is what unlocks the creative maximum value in others.

Gerry Arial

If someone is not doing her job, she will know it. If you talk and work with her on a daily basis, you can jointly come to the conclusion that she is in the wrong job. In my experience, some people agreed and some didn't. If you document, you are *not* trying to help. By the time it gets to documentation, you are going to fire someone unless an epiphany occurs.

Dave Dickson

The really effective influencers have far more power to lead to high performance than the processes they manage.

Shannon Tessier

When someone came into my office, I would make sure that they left with at least as many monkeys as they brought in, but not necessarily the same ones. People bring problems. When they come, they want to drop them off. Give them help and guidance but make sure that when they leave they go with direction *and* at least the same number of monkeys. There was a book a long time ago about this.

Dave Dickson

Leadership Rule #1

This leads us to what we consider to be the first of our three rules of applied leadership.

LEADERSHIP RULE #1
I promise to make you better, *and*
you promise to do your part.

This commitment cannot be silent. Every follower has the right to expect that his leader has specific plans to help him be better in all aspects of his work life.

Equally important, every follower has an obligation to do her part to live up to her promise, her values, her skill level. This mutual dependence leads to the second rule of applied leadership.

Leadership Rule #2

This second commitment seals the deal: mutually supporting promises that demand the leader and the follower have equal opportunity to challenge each other, when either the guidance or the growth is lacking. This commitment will make some a bit squeamish, we are sure, but as we like to tell our clients, "No one gets off the hook."

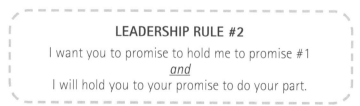

LEADERSHIP RULE #2
I want you to promise to hold me to promise #1
and
I will hold you to your promise to do your part.

There is a third rule, which we will talk about later. The good news for those who are intent on memorizing all this is that we think there are only three.

Getting back to the balancing of art and science, some simple but important functions require perspective. Both leadership art and management science are required to be successful. You need to find the right balance for you in your position in your organization.

You need to be able to recognize when it's not the plan
that's failing but the leadership applied to it.

Rosemarie Leclair

This is a big difference between management and leadership — a
leader will say, "One of the most important things, if not *the*
most important thing, is to sit and talk to my people." A manager
will say, "I have to do performance appraisals this week."

John Watts

Leadership trumps management. Our clients have leadership
expectations; therefore, coordination and management are not
sufficient for the value proposition. This is a little disturbing to some
who thought that coordination/management *was* the value proposition.

Franklin Holtforster

Situational credibility gives alignment to a common
cause. People have faith so long as they believe.

Franklin Holtforster

It isn't enough to hold yourself responsible as a leader or to exercise
your authority; you also need to hold yourself accountable. You
must accept the consequences of the leadership role you play.

Jean Boyle

ART AND SCIENCE

Leadership	*Management*
▶ Responsibility	▶ Plans
▶ Setting direction	▶ Budgets
▶ Aligning people	▶ Organization
▶ Stimulating activity	▶ Staffing methods
▶ Motivating	▶ Control and solving problems

LEADERSHIP ART *AND* MANAGEMENT SCIENCE

From a leadership perspective, the five functions shown above are absolutely required if high performance is your goal. Everyone you come into contact with needs to understand that you accept responsibility for your and your team's performance and the science that supports it. Your next obligation is to set the direction for your team, based on your translation of the challenges you face, and aligning team skills, interests, and potential as you go. In the action mode, your role is to stimulate new thinking, creativity, innovation, and the adaptability of your team members. Finally, you are the motivator — the one who provides hope and courage.

Here's an example of how we think one leader went about applying leadership in a crisis to create the best possible outcome.

Do you remember when one of Canada's new submarines had a tragic fire at sea resulting in a death? The submarine was towed back to port. Public criticism and finger pointing was instantaneous and constant. They wanted to know who was to blame. Why did we buy these submarines? Who trained this crew? What did they do wrong? One can only imagine how the crew felt and what stress they were under. In the centre of this storm, we believe it was the Commander of the Navy who decided to be dockside when the submarine made port. One might think that he was there to blame and criticize. We don't think he was. We watched the events unfold in a news clip. As each sailor left the submarine, the commander greeted him individually, sometimes with a hug, sometimes a pat on the shoulder, sometimes with a handshake. It was

Don't demand that your employees seek tacit permission to proceed. They don't need to ask for permission, if they understand the priorities and work within the boundaries of law, morality, etc.

Jan Kaminski

I can make others believe in a vision — as long as I believe in it. I can strive for that vision.

Deborah Dickson

Successful teams will know all that the leader knows and more. They will understand the context of things and won't have to be driven to perform. They will know what needs to get done, the quality expected, and they'll simply do it.

Gerry Arial

I think that the real leaders rely on character. It has to be natural and easy and honest, and they have genuine good intentions.

Rob Lindsay

A leader must foster an environment where people feel they can debate issues and that it is okay to have different perspectives, even if this means not always sharing the view of the boss.

France Jacovella

obvious to us that he was leading, taking responsibility, extending forgiveness, motivating. He was guaranteeing that this submarine crew would sail again, for all the right reasons. And they did.

Another example is a situation where Michael personally witnessed the delivery of all five of the leadership intentions. This occurred in the early seventies at a Canadian Forces Air Traffic Control unit in West Germany. This unit had all kinds of top-notch talent and had been recently re-equipped with the most modern air traffic control system that the Canadian Air Force had available. Despite what appeared to be the best possible opportunity for high performance, it seemed to him that the Air Traffic Control teams were underperforming, basically keeping things safe but not providing the level of air traffic control service that the combination of talent and equipment would have forecast. The Air Traffic Control teams just couldn't seem to get on the same page. There was more than enough frustration to go around.

A new senior air traffic control officer, Major Keith Cameron (later promoted to Lieutenant Colonel), came into this decidedly unhappy and underachieving team. Michael recalls what happened next.

The normal routine for the arriving officer was to take a few days to settle in and get the family in place. Keith instead sent us the first signal of his leadership style. He skipped the settling-in phase and immediately, after his transatlantic flight, went to the air traffic control centre. This visit was totally unexpected and unannounced. It sent a shiver through everyone. This was more than fresh air — it was an infusion of energy.

He literally burst into the main control room and within a few seconds asked everyone who was there to gather around. He introduced himself. He made it clear that he understood the frustrations of the past. In a very few words he accepted accountability for the past and declared responsibility for the future of the unit. He provided us his vision and he gave us the parameters within which we would work. For example, he made it clear that we would live up to the highest standards not only of air traffic control but also of military deportment, discipline, and involvement.

Different situations require different leadership strengths. For example, a leader might be really good at creating a vision and inspiring others, but might have to step aside for others to deliver. You need to know yourself well enough vis-à-vis your strengths and to understand where you need to be in leadership terms at any given time. Then, when you need help, reach out and get it!

Rosemarie Leclair

I remember when my Uncle Irving had passed away and I returned to Ottawa. I was visiting a model home we had built out in Hunt Club. It was a great model home, and I walked in and the Home Building Team was there. I walked through the house and pointed out seven or eight things that needed fixing, very minor, but needed fixing. We chatted some more, and I walked out. My brother Robert came running after me and was probably as angry as I'd ever seen him. I don't think he was going to punch me, but it was close. He was livid. He said, "What did you just do there?" I said, "About what? I just pointed out a few small things that were wrong." "Yes," Robert replied, "but you didn't point out the great many things that we did right. The people in there are practically in tears." I said, "But it's a great model!" and Robert replied, "So who would know that you feel that way?"

Roger Greenberg

I started to go to the general cafeteria for coffee and, one morning at 7.30 a.m., I bumped into a lineman. He's ahead of me in line buying coffee too. He says to the cash clerk, "Make that two." The clerk is looking at him and thinking, "He's going to buy the CEO a coffee." I could feel the wheels turning. I started to object to the lineman buying me a coffee, and he turned to me and said, "The way I see it, boss, you're doing a great job." I replied, "The way I see it, I get to go out and talk about the great job you guys are doing." He bought the coffee and we had a quick chat. I think we were influencing each other.

Rosemarie Leclair

The winds of change continued with this new leader, and within a year there had been a complete reversal. This air traffic control unit set the standard for high-performance air traffic and military excellence across all ranks. Of the people who were present during that time (only a very small segment of the whole air traffic control community), this unit produced a disproportionately high number of advancements in both technical and personnel terms. Out of this group came the designs for the next generation of radar and air traffic control concepts for Canada's military. Also, several of those people emerged from the Forces to lead successful private sector businesses. What was different about this group? It started with this one leader who showed them what was possible if they did it together with a clear and compelling vision.[2]

Leadership trumps management

Leadership is not just about the mechanics. It is not just about planning or managing your positions or budgets. Leaders do manage these things too,

---

SO WHAT?

Leadership art is NOT about:

strategic planning or annual planning or strategic review . . .

Leadership art IS about establishing:

- A leadership norm
- A culture
- Behaviours
- Mentoring
- Learning
- Understanding MVP
- Confidence
- Trust
- Permission
- Forgiveness
- A working value set (not just one for the wall)

Leaders establish the start line. Your leadership initiatives need nourishment — not fire and forget — the cycle, frequency, and content will depend on the progress of the leadership team as they adapt to and demonstrate the leadership norm.

Use the information in this book as a trigger to move yourself and your organization toward a leadership-based culture.

---

2   After a lengthy illness, Keith passed away recently. He is remembered by all who knew him as an inspirational air force officer and leader.

Change is happening so quickly now, at a pace that is uncertain. In some cases your decisions may rip the heart out of the organization — killing the spirit. But on the other hand you need to take those decisions to enable growth and innovation.

Jim Orban

—————————————————

Leaders must change with the times. Thirty to forty years ago times changed every fifteen to twenty years. Now they change every nine months. The rate of change has increased so leaders must be able to adapt themselves and then get their people to change, too. Henry Ford had a marketing plan whereby you could have any colour of car so long as it was black. He could not exist today.

Dave Dickson

—————————————————

If the leader doesn't take the tough decisions along with the more pleasant things, the outcome will suffer; believe me, I've been there. The reality is . . . the reality!

Jim Durrell

—————————————————

If you want people to do more than just the minimum, you have to understand what is important to them. If you understand their values, you have a better chance at getting their commitment.

France Jacovella

but leadership input provides so much more. Leadership establishes a vision and a culture of values, behaviours, and norms that continually provide followers with the commitment and courage to be the best they can be. It "frames" their effort.

As a leader, you must establish the ground rules under which you operate and that you expect others to follow. Your objective is to determine your leadership framework for each leading situation you find yourself in. The context may be different, but some things do not normally change: trust, forgiveness, responsibility, permission, and your value set.

Your vision will and must change as your environment changes. If you change your values and behaviours, however, you will be found out. You will not be credible to those around you. You will be known; the question is, what do you want to be known for?

Twenty-first-century context

There is no doubt that leadership must work, because no amount of process, procedure, and rule enforcement can cope with the tsunami of change that we are experiencing in the twenty-first century. How could you know the rates of change would impact your life and the world so dramatically? How could you know that the faith we had put into conventional business practices would prove to be, in some cases, misdirected?

HIGH RATES OF CHANGE

How could you know:

▶ That the auto industry would be in such turmoil?

▶ That Ontario would be a have-not province?

▶ That governments around the world would be bailing out major banks?

▶ That interest rates would be the lowest in memory?

▶ That Canada would designate a "Highway of Heroes"?

▶ That the economic engine of the world would move to China?

▶ And many others . . .

Situational credibility has two parts: the assumed authority that is inherent in a role and the maintained authority — remaining authoritative, being well informed, keeping the company aligned to a common cause, and identifying and keeping aligned to values.

Franklin Holtforster

Get outside your comfort zone if your intention is real change!

Jean Boyle

This generation has a need to generate job satisfaction from clear challenges balanced with a strong personal life. This, to some, is a new dynamic, which means that leaders have to understand that for each worker, there may be a different set of buttons to push. Maybe we need to have pools of employees to match with different requirements.

Rosemarie Leclair

In my business, the economic uncertainty creates a real fear in people. But I know that they are watching me, so I come in with a big, bold smile. I stay positive, but I don't sugar-coat our challenges. My team understands that the sun will rise again, and if we keep doing what we all need to, we'll be here waiting when it does. That's our goal.

Jim Durrell

At these times, when everyone is apparently talking at once, bombarding us with ever more information, it is difficult to separate what is important from the noise around us. To say that we missed the significance of the lessons we should have learned from the events of the past ten to fifteen years would be a gross understatement.

WHAT HAS CHANGED?

▶ *Nineteenth-century concepts that have been the rule even in the twentieth century.*
What were the socio-economic/geopolitical circumstances in the nineteenth and twentieth centuries that defined and dominated workplace behaviour and structure?

▶ *The characteristics of this kind of workplace.*
Relationships tended to be linear, work centres around population mass, lots of change but a low change rate, conforming, long-standing paradigms, relatively low info change rate, low education and learning rates, relatively stable, human and individual rights restrictions, restrictions of personal and info movement, process-dependent. Could we be *any* more different in *every* area today?

Business practices today are founded in the lessons learned from the past hundred and fifty years. Although we acknowledge that we are generalizing a bit, we believe that the most relevant lessons have occurred from the industrial revolution forward. We need to look to the past forty years to find the genesis of the current leadership challenge: the emergence of a global economy, the information age, the collapse of communism in Europe, the emergence of China and India as buying and selling giants, the economic collapse of 2008, and the looming environmental crisis.[3]

---

3   Thomas L. Friedman, *The World Is Flat (A Brief History of the Twenty-First Century)* (New York: Farrar, Straus, and Giroux, 2006).

This is not a time to be thinking you can get it all done by yourself. It's clear to me that you can't!

Rosemarie Leclair

Really good leaders lead with their heads *and* with their hearts. On the one hand, you can say a leader must inspire, motivate, and, above all else, be a good communicator. On the other hand, you have to have an ability to know the best way forward in an increasingly ambiguous environment.

Jim Orban

The new world economy and globalization did not happen because of governments, it happened in spite of governments! This is the people talking, with their demand for work and health care and consumer products. You have to be able to manage an increasing complexity, and perhaps active leadership provides the grease for that to happen.

J-P Soublière

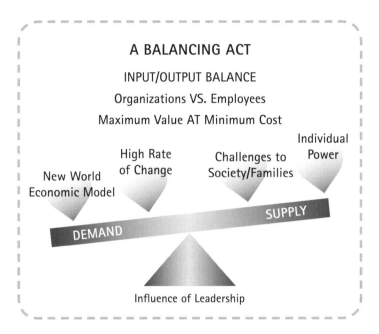

These events have created rates of change in the workplace that have outstripped the ability of many organizations to adapt. At the individual level, the consequence of these changes and the failure of organizations to adapt to them has been displacement, function/skill misalignment, and disengagement.

Another consequence is the disappearance of "linear employment," where we expected to stay with and advance with the same organization for the duration of our careers. In this century, career agility has turned out to be everything.

Further complicating the workplace are the demands of the organization versus the needs of the individual.

Organizations want maximum value at minimum cost, an overall, better "bottom line." Individuals are looking for worthwhile employment, purpose, and the satisfaction of their emotional and physical needs. These are often competing interests. Most individuals are looking for opportunities to be the best they can be in an environment where there is some sharing of purpose, value, and intention. Our research with proven leaders reveals that when we are leading effectively, we are capable of achieving both, at the expense of neither.

When I see people with leadership potential, I make sure they know they have a future that is beyond what they may be doing, that they have the capacity to lead. But they have to take action to make this capability grow. These employees will have to prove themselves tough enough to lead or will they fold and fade away.

Jim Durrell

I believe that leadership characteristics are like economics. There are core economic indicators and then there are the variables. The variables can cause inflation to go up or down. I think the same applies to leadership. As long as you have that core set of characteristics — being smarter, being able to motivate, communicate, etc. — you have the potential. You don't have to have all of them to the hilt, but you have to have some semblance of the core.

Jim Orban

I believe that every one of my employees has unique properties that allow them to be seen and behave in some high-value way. My role is to set the example and to try to stretch myself to understand how I can help them reach just a bit higher each day.

Gerry Arial

It is easier to have good and strong relationship with the great performers. They get a lot of the high-profile files and therefore more exchange of ideas, more meetings, more opportunity to replace me when I am away, and more opportunity to get discovered and known. Dealing with poor performers is much more difficult, especially when there are differences in the value system. When someone is willing to improve, to learn, and adjust, it is important to invest the time and effort. It is important to realize, however, that if the plan for improvement does not work, then sometimes people need to be let go.

France Jacovella

To provide some context for the transition from the old workplace to the twenty-first-century version, we have developed a possible effect of the application of the maximum value proposition, shown in the diagram that follows.

Below on the left is our approximation of the distribution of organizational effort as it was. To get from the former organization model to the one demanded in this century (on the right) requires intentional effort to change with the power of leadership "leading the way." It is not conceivable to us to think that our working population can juggle all the pressures of change in our society – economic, familial, societal, community – without finding their way to their highest performance level.

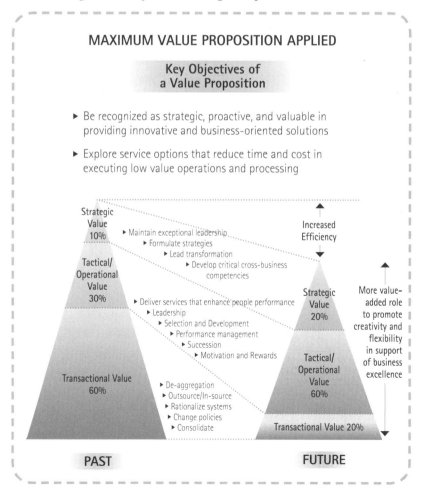

MAXIMUM VALUE PROPOSITION APPLIED

Key Objectives of a Value Proposition

▸ Be recognized as strategic, proactive, and valuable in providing innovative and business-oriented solutions

▸ Explore service options that reduce time and cost in executing low value operations and processing

Strategic Value 10%
▸ Maintain exceptional leadership
▸ Formulate strategies
▸ Lead transformation
▸ Develop critical cross-business competencies

Tactical/ Operational Value 30%
▸ Deliver services that enhance people performance
▸ Leadership
▸ Selection and Development
▸ Performance management
▸ Succession
▸ Motivation and Rewards

Transactional Value 60%
▸ De-aggregation
▸ Outsource/In-source
▸ Rationalize systems
▸ Change policies
▸ Consolidate

Increased Efficiency

Strategic Value 20%

Tactical/ Operational Value 60%

Transactional Value 20%

More value-added role to promote creativity and flexibility in support of business excellence

PAST

FUTURE

People are capable of much more than they think. If you don't think you are capable, you won't become capable. To never have known what you are capable of only because you didn't know better is an absolute shame.

Franklin Holtforster

Trying to get all these capabilities in balance is not easy. It's not just charisma — if it were, you would go into politics. It's how those pieces work together in balance.

John Watts

In my experience, I have had only limited success in changing people to make them more valuable when their spots were already fixed in a negative pattern.

Rob Lindsay

The growing process presents a picture that is almost "messy." This may be a characteristic of the process — leadership is messy . . .

Jan Kaminski

In today's organizations, where there is one crisis after another, still another project after the last one, and yet another business plan or year-end to get through, it can be hard on staff to be at maximum value all of the time. You need to provide some relief through various means (assignment, rotating leadership, etc.) to promote health and maximum vitality — to be ready for the next push. Leaders must recognize this and consciously allow for it.

Deborah Dickson

One sure way to get there is for leaders at all levels to accept their responsibilities and to create the right kind of environment for this performance to be realized.

MEETING THE CHALLENGE

Twenty-first-century workplace realities:

▶ Max flex (volatile and unstable)

▶ Non-linear

▶ Individual

▶ Change-driven, innovation required, speed essential

▶ High learning rates

▶ Non-conforming, high info and intellectual transfer rates

▶ Vision-driven

▶ Leadership-dependent (energy/courage)

*Outstanding leaders appeal to the hearts
of their followers, not their minds!*

The applied leadership high performer or team rises to meet the twenty-first-century challenge. They are able to adjust to instability and volatility by maintaining a hold on values and behaviour. Even though they may be in a non-linear relationship with their organization, individual leaders have clear intentions, and everyone feels they belong.

The shared agreement on behaviour is important and promotes maximum speed with minimal interference. The permission/forgiveness agreement allows the nonconforming individual to still fit in. The constant encouragement by the applied leader transfers energy and courage to the high-performing team. From everything we have found over the past three years, leaders and teams behaving this way are the best inoculation against twenty-first-century failure.

There should be a "Leadership Law of Reciprocity." When someone really makes a great contribution, the leader must reciprocate by at least acknowledging the success. Do not budget your congratulatory messages.

Shannon Tessier

The best of leaders stand on the highest of mountains and in the most public way proclaim the successes of those who achieve their results, but go to the quietest of small rooms to criticize the work of a few.

Roger Greenberg

When my employees get it wrong, when we don't meet the commitment to our customers or the quality I expect, we fix the problem together, as a team. This I think is an approach that encourages employees to hang in when times are bad. We are in this together and I won't abandon them.

Gerry Arial

I understand my soft spots and one of them is dealing with employees when things go wrong. I've learned that even though it's uncomfortable, in those cases, it is *because* it's uncomfortable that I need to do it. The leader needs to get out of the comfort zone if real change is to happen.

Rob Lindsay

When your leadership produces great results and you are moving forward, with poor performers leaving as you go, establish an approach that ensures that your new believers are welcomed as equal partners. You'll need them to want to be there, performing by choice.

Rosemarie Leclair

Leadership Rule #3

LEADERSHIP RULE #3

I promise to celebrate our successes
in public and discuss our failures in private
and I ask you to do the same.

Our first two rules are the *grease* that enables things to happen. The leader improves others. Others do their part. Both sides agree to hold each other accountable.

Leadership Rule #3 is more about the *glue* to hold things together. Celebrations in public promote pride in effort by individuals and groups. Celebrations provide resilience in tough times. Celebrations splatter across the organization to those who have not yet achieved what they have set out to do – encouraging and motivating them to continue. Celebrations promote emotional connections and commitment and increase loyalty, while neutralizing negativity from marginal performers.

The commitment to discuss failures in private (at the request of either the leader or the follower) guarantees the opportunity to repair damage, learn lessons, resolve misunderstandings, reinforce values and behaviours, and regain confidence and momentum.

From our experience, you might get away with being less than diligent with leadership rules 1 and 2 and still recover. But if you violate rule 3, you are courting disaster.

The individual employee today will not tolerate public criticism, humiliation, and punishment when he/she was looking for high-performance commitment and loyalty. You will be toast.

We have talked about the twenty-first-century context and the factors that have led up to the situation we find ourselves in today.

The way we see it, the economic and personal factors are more or less outside of a leader's control. On the other hand, if you bring to bear your leadership presence; establish value, vision, and behaviour norms; and then deliberately and purposefully apply the leadership rules, you can create an environment

My uncle Irving and my father provided completely different and contrasting styles of leadership. Irving was a bombastic, highly intelligent and brilliant leader. You'd sit with him and at times he would be so loud, you would be recoiling. My father was quiet and composed and led by applying his dogged determination on the administration side. From an overall point of view, the two of them worked together very effectively.

Roger Greenberg

— — — — — — — — — — — — — — — — — —

Leadership is the catalyst to great performance. Performance is realized by understanding the goals, having clear accountability as to whose goal it is, and planning how it's going to be accomplished. Everybody has to buy into these principles.

John Watts

— — — — — — — — — — — — — — — — — —

Attentive leaders recognize the power of the individual. Individuals can bring companies down or build them up.

Jim Orban

where team members can deploy their best effort *while maintaining their independence and flexibility.* Not only will you ride the storm out, you will have gained both technical and strategic advantage. You will see long-term performance gains.

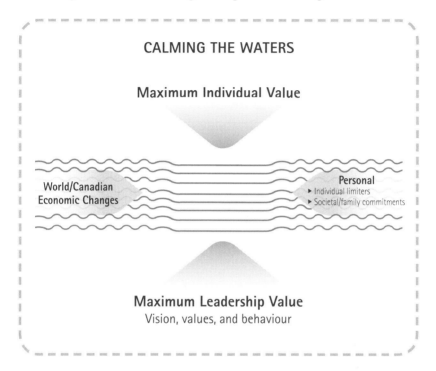

CALMING THE WATERS

Maximum Individual Value

World/Canadian
Economic Changes

Personal
▸ Individual limiters
▸ Societal/family commitments

Maximum Leadership Value
Vision, values, and behaviour

SECTION TWO

Finding Your Leadership "Centre"

Your leadership "centre" is the core of your leadership foundation and is the source of your natural leadership influence. When you are behaving in "sync" with this "centre" you will have the energy to lead and the maximum opportunity to influence others.

This leadership centre has several components, including your understanding and style of leadership, the application of your MVP, and the steps you need to take to develop your leadership cultural framework.

Let's take a look at some key information and ideas to explore and build your leadership foundation.

Leadership basics

The U.S. Army runs one of its advertising campaigns based on the notion that every soldier is an "Army of One." They don't mean that everyone is capable of doing everything. They mean that everyone needs to be in command of him/herself. They are telling us that all soldiers have the responsibility to be "The Best That They Can Be" (another theme they use).

> **LEADERSHIP BASICS**
>
> Employees survive and prosper when:
> ▸ They have career control
> ▸ They can perform to their maximum value

Obviously you would have to use the right examples
and tone depending on your audience, but leadership
is leadership regardless of the generation!

On the other hand, appealing to groups can be humbling. I was
speaking to a high school group, the boys in the back, the girls up
front, and I thought I was really doing well with my message. After
the speech I asked if there were any questions. A girl in the front
had been listening to me rapturously and leaped to her feet and
said "Mayor Holzman, we just loved . . . we just loved your belt!"

That brought me down a notch or two, but you
know, I wore that belt for weeks after that!

Jacquelin Holzman

— — — — — — — — — — — — — — — — — —

Leading and deciding to do things is great, but you'd better
have the guts to admit when you've blown something and
you'd better have saved the energy to start again.

Jean Boyle

— — — — — — — — — — — — — — — — — —

If you look at people that fail in a leadership situation, it is not
that they are failed leaders — everyone can lead to a certain
context. From a business context, it was because they couldn't
create that situational credibility or they couldn't get the follower-
ship in place. They didn't really think about what it took.

Jan Kaminski

— — — — — — — — — — — — — — — — — —

Leadership brings its burdens, too. You have to take the
time to know yourself, your boundaries, limits, strengths,
and, of course, your areas for more development.

Shannon Tessier

There are many organizations that operate in accordance with the same principle. All of our interviewees operate under this principle in their day-to-day relationships with their teams. For teams to be successful, they must be filled with people who individually believe that they can control their career progress and that they are capable of performing at some self-identified view of their maximum value.

When we present this idea to transition clients at KWA Partners (Ottawa) Limited, sometimes their reaction is one of surprise. When they realize that they are responsible for themselves, then they do take career control, and their transition period ends, one way or another. This may just be a state of mind but it points out to us how powerful to the individual is the connection between career control and satisfactory employment.

Once achieved, the control is not enough. It is simply the starting point for the individual to explore what she knows, what she wants, what her MVP might be, who she really is, and what she stands for. This exploration usually leads to an understanding by the individual of not just what she represents to others, but how to express it. It is during this phase that she becomes comfortable with who she is and she becomes attractive to others as a potential resource. At this point she is ready to be led or to lead.

THE APPLIED LEADERSHIP PRESCRIPTION . . .

- ▶ A leader's relationship:
  - ▸ Is direct
  - ▸ Is intentional
  - ▸ Influences to an outcome
- ▶ The team, including the leader, operates from:
  - ▸ A set of common values, principles, and behaviours
- ▶ Together they move toward a common vision, translated into team language, understood at all levels.

Check your ego at the door. Make it a habit to make your leadership style one that blends in with every one of your staff.

Rosemarie Leclair

— — — — — — — — — — — — — — — — — —

I want to know that recruits are upwardly mobile, not just happy in one job. A waiter who doesn't want to be a manager must want to be the best waiter in the world and he must understand what that means. For people like this who do not want to progress, make sure you don't put them into a position where they create a bottleneck for others. These types of people can make good trainers for those on their way up.

Dave Dickson

— — — — — — — — — — — — — — — — — —

Every leader should be building his/her own leadership network. Learn from others, find the shortcuts already practised and proven by others.

Rosemarie Leclair

— — — — — — — — — — — — — — — — — —

You have to lead in all directions. One of my bosses was very good at leading upwards. I think that was his complete focus. And I think that is a mistake. I suppose it's just as big a mistake to lead downward and not look up. You have to look in all directions.

John Watts

Our evidence is based on experience, not theory. We know that when individuals reach this state of control and MVP, there is a direct and positive effect in their workplace. They may use fewer sick days, reach or exceed deliverables or quotas more easily, have fewer grievances, stay more focused, and generally enjoy their work more. At its most basic level, this is the "army of one" but the effect in a team setting when applied leadership is present is exponential. When we meet teams who are clearly at the peak of their power, we find dedicated leaders who are often following the same basic prescription:

- ▶ Get career control!
- ▶ Find your maximum value.
- ▶ Use your MVP.

Getting your act together

How do you find and then move to your maximum value? Here are the steps that will help you understand yourself and help prepare you to move ahead.

Step 1: Determine your sense of urgency. Determine in your own mind how urgent it is to embrace a high-performance leadership approach. Do you think that adopting applied leadership ideas could lead you to higher performance, more rewards, better contentment? If you honestly do sense the urgency, then you can do something to move toward those goals.

Step 2: Know where you come from. Conduct a full review of your personal history. Write it down. Look at significant events in your life and how those events affected your outlook. Be honest about it. Stay balanced. Spend as much time reviewing your successes as your failures. You are looking for the lessons.

There are some wonderful books that can help you with this journey: for example, Marge Watters's *It's Your Move*,[4] while designed for transition challenges, has some wonderful and easy to complete exercises that will help you think about and document your personal history.

---

4   Marge Watters, *It's Your Move* (Toronto: HarperCollins Canada Ltd., 2001).

Mentorship is a responsibility of leaders. I check in regularly with new hires. I try to understand where their heads are at, and what can be done differently. I remind them not to abandon their previous experience. It's a two-way street. It is their responsibility, too. They have to say what they are seeing as well.

Jim Orban

- - - - - - - - - - - - - - - - - - - -

As a leader in my profession, I understand clearly that I must share my knowledge if we are to push the capability envelope of employees, or those who are simply learning our craft. If I don't, if we don't, we simply stand still.

Gerry Arial

- - - - - - - - - - - - - - - - - - - -

I get the most out of my leadership when I see that I'm able to make people feel good about themselves. This could be a work or personal issue, it makes no difference to me.

Rob Lindsay

- - - - - - - - - - - - - - - - - - - -

In the absence of leadership, people will rise to the challenge and become leaders and advocates in a group. Recognize this in the environment you are in. There are times when this style of pragmatic leadership will get things done. Know who the influencers are and keep in touch with them.

Jim Orban

Step 3: Know who you are. There are excellent assessment tools that are available in any bookstore or on-line that will provide a picture of your interests, skills, personality, preferences, likes, dislikes, and values. Use as many of these as you need to form a picture that you are comfortable with and able to talk about. In the end, you need to know and be able to express not only who you are, but what you stand for. Refer to Appendix D for a sample of self-assessment tools.

Step 4: Build a leadership coalition. A leadership coalition is a group of like-minded people who get together to share and discuss issues, ideas, and opportunities. They share fundamental values and principles, can communicate easily, and can be trusted to give us perspective and guidance. It could be a social, a business, or a sports network. Everyone in it must know its purpose and be there by choice.

BUILDING A COALITION

Whom do you know?
Whom do you trust?
Whom do you value?
Whom do you confide in?
Whom do you learn from?
Who will be honest with you?
Who has strengths to complement your weaknesses?

A leadership coalition can be a powerful tool to help understand and consolidate your MVP and provide a forum for discussion on how to deploy it. It could also provide guidance and insight when you or someone else is facing difficult or challenging situations. It also provides the power of a network to promote members' MVP outside the coalition.

Determine who meets the criteria. Secure their agreement to belong and make sure there is agreement about the purpose. Prepare for meetings. Have intent — bring items for the agenda. Create a structure for your coalition — a regular meeting time, location, etc. Make it fun and provide some value to others. Coalition members will want to contribute

On a leader's first day on the job, it might not be ideal to line up all the direct reports and say, "Look to the right, look to the left, six months from now one of you won't be here anymore." This isn't exactly a sensible comment to elicit the support, collaboration, and initiative that one would expect.

Rosemarie Leclair

— — — — — — — — — — — — — — — —

To enable people to do what they are really capable of doing, the leader needs to give them the opportunity to make mistakes. Leaders must recognize that mistakes do happen and that you will not necessarily get it right the first time.

France Jacovella

— — — — — — — — — — — — — — — —

One of my first bosses taught me basic principles, such as, "You can't fight with a skunk and come out smelling good yourself."

J-P Soublière

— — — — — — — — — — — — — — — —

You must replace yourself! It may be the first thing you do for yourself, for your staff, and for your boss. I learned this later in my career. I think also that it's important that people around you know that is your plan! You need to be finding and leading other leaders — developing them and delegating to them — so they'll learn.

Jacquelin Holzman

when they know it is something they value. It is a reciprocal agreement that all members benefit from.

Step 5 – Find opportunities to activate your MVP. You may or may not have the opportunity to use your MVP in your everyday work. Perhaps your unique capacity to influence others is not something your workplace needs you to be using. Perhaps you are a naturally strong communicator or an exceptional planner without a stage for using these skills. Your first step is to make sure that you use and promote your MVP in your organization. Find ways to contribute, even if it is not in your job description. Have a conversation with your boss. Summarize what you know about yourself. Offer suggestions on how you can help. Take control of your MVP. There are limitless opportunities outside of work, too. Volunteer wherever you have an interest.

These five steps will help you to recognize and use your MVP. They prepare you for high performance as an individual, whether you work as part of a team or on your own.

Team basics

Most of us work in some form of team environment. Applied leadership is crucial to team success. And team success is crucial to organizational success.

LEADERSHIP INTEGRATES AND BUILDS . . .

Individual Value → Team Performance → Management Excellence → Organizational Success

Strong leaders at the lower level are going to shine no matter
what is happening above. You get way better performance
there if the people at the top are living it. You get broader
acceptance, performance, training, and awareness.

Jan Kaminski

To make an organization nimble enough to cope successfully
with the change dynamic requires a leadership style that focuses
on translating future needs and communicating them to the
workers so that they can adjust and cope without filling every
day with micro-instructions. There is no time for that.

Rosemarie Leclair

People will make mistakes and you have to let them.
You have to spend the time and say, "What did you
do wrong and what are the lessons learned?"

John Watts

Good leaders instinctively recognize the reality of the situation
and have the ability to transmit the reality, while at the same
time inspiring the correct action. If strong relationships are
already in place, then the communication strikes home.

Jim Durrell

*LEADERSHIP IS THE GREASE THAT ALLOWS US TO MOVE
from individual, to team, to management, to organizational
SUCCESS.*

Nothing about this progression is accidental. Individuals who truly understand and deploy their individual MVP within well-defined teams and management structures that make sense dominate successful organizations. These same organizations are incapable of excellence if any one part of the inner circle is dysfunctional, undefined, or ignored. This becomes a mutually supporting mechanism for high performance when all the parts are working.

Before we get into the details of how applied leadership can build successful team performance, let's talk briefly about leadership styles. To do this we must introduce some basic leadership theory with respect to styles.

There are six main leadership styles that are generally acknowledged to exist. There is an appropriate time and place for each of them to be used. This is a challenge for any leader. Within our individual MVP, we often have preferences for one style over the other, even when it isn't appropriate or best for the situation. Let's explore some of the choices.

LEADERSHIP STYLES

- ▶ Coercive (demands immediate compliance)
- ▶ Authoritative (mobilizes toward a vision)
- ▶ Collaborative (creates harmony and bonds)
- ▶ Democratic (forges consensus)
- ▶ Pacesetting (sets high standards)
- ▶ Coaching (develops people for the future)

Coercive. In our opinion, a coercive leadership style would, in most circumstances, be not only inappropriate but, extended over a period of time, would be destructive to the team. Coercive behaviour is aggressive, manipulative, very directive, and is based on a punishment principle. The classic line is "Do this

Civility is part of leadership. I despise people who kiss up and spit down. I do not tolerate a lack of respect, and just because you are a senior manager, you cannot treat people below you badly.

Jim Orban

There are times when a decision must be made quickly and consultation is not feasible or wise.

France Jacovella

Throughout my professional life I have tried to be reasonable and fair with people. When you face having to deal with those in life and in business who are simply not nice, you have to walk away. When things are going wrong, when there are issues to be resolved, go to the people, explain to them the choices and options, and throughout be respectful, be nice! No one is perfect, but there is no need to go to battle. No one wins then, in the long run.

J-P Soublière

Although there are all kinds and varieties of leaders and leadership styles, beware of the authoritative pacesetters. I had one on my staff once and almost lost all of the other team members over time. They left exhausted and tired and disheartened. I finally realized what was happening and my pacesetter had to move on.

Gerry Arial

or else" – the "or else" often implied, not stated. It tends to isolate the more timid or weaker members. Of course, if the building is on fire, you might want to react quickly to the "get out or else" order.

Authoritative. An authoritative leadership style when used appropriately is a good and often necessary approach. There are times when a leader must exert his or her authority and specifically direct action to accomplish a necessary and high-priority task. Overuse or unnecessary use will breed resistance, or worse: disengagement. Directed solutions are devoid of opportunity for creativity and growth. In our experience, in the long run, the leader who uses the authoritative approach excessively dismisses the possibility of using the full MVP of his or her team.

Collaborative. In a collaborative and co-operative workplace, the affiliative leader delivers on the promise of human value and harmony. This leadership style is particularly useful in organizations where operations are focused on helping others and improving the human condition. Teams in these kinds of organizations are particularly effective when the leadership style mirrors the team's interest in helping others (in a literal sense).

Despite the agreeableness and intuitive value of this leadership style, there are dangers. First, to use this style exclusively is to ignore the leader's obligation to set expectations and to always strive for the best solution rather than the common denominator of harmony and bonding. Second, the affiliative leader is often subject to the agenda of the needy team member. It is difficult to be seen to be at the head of the parade, leading the way, if most of your time is spent at the back of the parade trying to appease and create harmony. This might be an appropriate time to point out that sometimes to be leading is to be lonely.

Democratic. The democratic leadership style displays an interest in getting the whole team on board, with consensus for decisions, as they move forward. Like the other leadership styles, there are times and circumstances when the democratic style is exactly what the doctor ordered. This is a clear case of making sure that you pick the right circumstances.

The difference between the follower and the leader is smaller than many leaders would like to think.

Franklin Holtforster

— — — — — — — — — — — — — — — — —

When your messages get right to those who do the job, you're influencing directly. Find out why things aren't working and identify those (put a light on them) who are accountable. Reassure them, but they need to change! Establish red-tape-cutting teams who can shepherd the changes.

Jacquelin Holzman

— — — — — — — — — — — — — — — —

There is no doubt in my mind that leadership skills are learned. There must be an evolution of leadership and experience growth so that others will accept your credibility when you take the lead. In other words, they'll follow.

Jean Boyle

— — — — — — — — — — — — — — — —

I think leadership is a blessing for me personally. I don't have to work nearly as hard, because I now practise leadership. I used to work six and a half days a week. And I don't think I had good self-awareness. I was just doing work. I was managing. I was administering.

Jan Kaminski

Your team needs to know that their collective voice is heard. And you need to provide regular opportunities to listen. The democratic leader really understands the power of this dynamic but is also able to be the final arbiter and move smoothly into the authoritative style to close the deal. There are occasions when this leader simply needs to trust the consensus to solve a challenge. Examples might be: how the team would support a local charity; or how the team would take care of one of its own in times of need; or perhaps simply how to decorate the office. These issues are not minor, although they might appear at first glance to be. How the team sees itself reflected in its surroundings and its social behaviours will be a critical component of its identity and collective MVP.

Pacesetting. The pacesetter is the leader who sets high expectations and who lives by those high expectations in his professional and personal life. Who could argue with this approach? The negative aspect of this approach to leadership is the implication that everyone except the leader is inadequate, unprepared, or not measuring up. This unfortunately is the general effect on teams of the overly enthusiastic and passionate pacesetter.

You will recognize the pacesetter because he never recognizes the limitations of anyone as being reasonable and human. There are certainly situations where a pacesetter is the one you want in charge, but in the long term the pacesetters that we have known have lived by a scorched-earth approach that achieved momentary greatness followed by long-term damage. Pacesetters find it hard to live by Leadership Rule #1. They don't develop others. They simply expect others and themselves to perform at extraordinary levels continuously. A code blue team in an emergency department at a hospital might be a good example of a positive pacesetting team. Extended throughout the hospital, however, this approach would be untenable.

Coaching. The leader who embraces a coaching style is one who is focused on Leadership Rule #1. As in the other examples, there are times when the "leader coach" will need to select a more appropriate style for the circumstances within which she finds herself. But, for the most part, this is the style most likely

Although the leader needs to encourage new behaviours, new efforts, new challenges and tasks, the encouragement must be offered in sensible ways. It won't work to simply throw everything out there. You need to know your employees' strengths and interests and then cut the cloth to fit.

Shannon Tessier

Unless the vision is translated into digestible bits, all committed, we will never be able to bring meaning to the average employee's day on the job. Top-down clear leadership makes this possible.

Rosemarie Leclair

The right words or talk aren't good enough. I have found that sometimes those who shout the loudest about high moral principles may be the greatest frauds of all.

Roger Greenberg

A senior executive I admired used to sit and talk with all sorts of people from the manufacturing floor to the executive offices. He always treated everyone as a unique individual — there were no differences in value between people. That is something I have picked up and have used for over thirty years.

John Watts

Often leadership skills have a lifespan, a period of maximum effectiveness. But even when the leader is not operating at his or her maximum, it doesn't mean that he/she is not influencing. In fact, this may be the time to start bringing others forward to lead.

Jim Durrell

to promote long-term success in the twenty-first-century high-performance team. The reason is simple. The rates of change that we have already discussed and the changing circumstances of employees and teams require a leadership style that draws on the strengths – and mediates the weaknesses – of everyone.

This is classic coaching. Sports teams that win championships are rarely the teams with the most aggregate talent. The champions come from those teams where strong and purposeful coaching has integrated individuals to the point where the sum is greater than the parts, *more than the science would have predicted.*

From our perspective, the coaching style is the one that is most likely of all to create the best long-term results, with the added benefit of attracting the best candidates and keeping them moving forward. If you are looking for a leadership style for yourself, invest in learning the best coaching practices and behaviours. It may not be perfect for all situations but it will get you most of the performance you need without the major negative issues that some of the other styles produce.

The energy to lead

Leaders need to be passionate, enthusiastic, available, flexible, open, and forthright . . . *all the time.* It's exhausting to think about it.

Your MVP, once you know and understand it, includes a positive energy balance that allows you to project your leadership style and characteristics in a consistent and authentic way. This energy projection is a challenge.

Often we find ourselves in specific challenging situations or involved with a continuous series of events in which we are projecting our style – leading – and often receiving little in immediate return to replenish our energy. Energy we need for the next crisis.

I learned from a former boss that while we need to
get all the tasks done, we also need a life!

Rob Lindsay

— — — — — — — — — — — — — — — —

A basic rule I use is, find the optimists and work with them. In addition,
you need people to challenge you. If you can combine the two, you've
really got something — a positive, optimistic, assertive employee.

J-P Soublière

— — — — — — — — — — — — — — — —

In our organization, people are given the responsibility and
the authority to lead with respect to the domain they own.
Everyone entirely understands this. It is an empowering
organization. Giving people responsibility for their work allows
them to take discretionary control over what they do. Giving
people responsibility is enabling and reduces stress.

Franklin Holtforster

— — — — — — — — — — — — — — — —

Despite our inclination to reach out to others to pull them
up, to offer help, we have to draw the line when we are
burning up almost all our energy helping the lowest member.
The high performers need our support as well.

Shannon Tessier

— — — — — — — — — — — — — — — —

My personal belief is that you can always lead something for
a finite period of time. You will run out of leadership energy,
that fire in your belly, and become ineffective as a leader.
That fire is different for everyone, its power, its length. When
your fire is waning, then it's time to find new challenges.

Jim Durrell

Part of your MVP is what we call your "getting by line." This is the level at which you can cope. When the leadership challenges you face drive your energy below this line, your ability to absorb more challenges, your ability to re-energize, your ability to influence in a healthy and positive way will be diminished – perhaps to a point where your outlook is reactive and negative. These are not the characteristics you are aiming for.

Your getting by line is set through the combination of three things: your genetic framework – your inherited abilities; the lessons learned or confidence gained from the nurturing part of your life; and your decisions and their consequences in all aspects of your adult life.

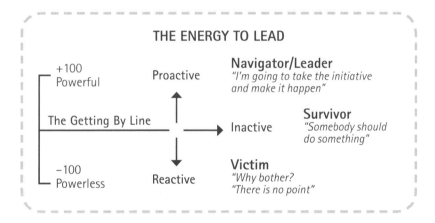

The diagram above illustrates the possible effects that depleted or refreshed energy levels can present. It is very important that you understand what fills you up and what drains you.

Listen to your mind and body. Know when you are full or getting near empty. Know what the symptoms are and trust them. You cannot lead successfully over the long haul unless you have the required energy stored or regularly replenished. Your followers will certainly know and they are counting on you.

There are assessments you can use to help you understand what your tolerance levels are and what your major risk and

I was working as a manager in a flower shop where the son of the owner, a business graduate, took over the business and started to apply more science to the process. More profit, more weddings, more flower orders were the goals. That's fine, but the only way we could do this was to lower the quality, the creativity, and so on. I learned all the techniques, and soon we had become a factory, turning out masses of flower arrangements without meeting the details of the customer's needs. I'm not saying that this was wrong, but it certainly was wrong for me.

Gerry Arial

It's fundamental: the leader needs to know what is intended, otherwise . . .

Rosemarie Leclair

I have been in situations where although the people were really good and meant well, they were tired and had stopped moving forward. When that happens, the leader rebuilds, re-energizes, and refocuses the effort. When I rebuild, I look for those who really enjoy teamwork rather than those who look for individual leadership roles. This helps get the focus right without tripping over egos.

Jim Durrell.

The real issue is always "doing the right thing." It may not even be important to do it really well, but just to do it! I think that there are many "right things" that just don't get done because we get sidetracked with all the other stuff.

J-P Soublière

replenishment activities might be. See Appendix D at the end of this book.

One thing that is important to understand about your energy level is that it can be replenished on a continuous basis by acknowledging the small victories in your everyday life. Examples: simply setting a schedule and keeping it, being kind and courteous to others, identifying bite-sized tasks, activating the celebration factor in Leadership Rule #3 by acknowledging someone else's achievement, or a thousand other things. Whatever you think it might take for you to maintain a positive energy balance, it is always worth it, especially when you don't feel like it. Energy balance is a key to maintaining your authentic self. It is your authentic self that displays your MVP.

A practical leadership model

In 1987, Michael attended a strategic planning conference that led to his first epiphany on leadership. Although he had been in uniform for twenty-five years at that time and thought he knew something about leadership, if he was going to be honest, he would have had to say that sometimes leadership was just as mysterious to him then as the day he joined the air force.

At the planning conference, during the lunch break, a psychologist who was a guest speaker made a presentation on problem solving. Hardly anyone was paying attention. The noise in the room (plates, knives, conversations) was distracting. Michael may have been the only one who really heard what he was saying. In the course of the presentation, the speaker talked about his various corporate clients and the problems he had solved for them. At one point he summarized his observation about leaders who weren't achieving the right level of performance: "They don't seem to grasp that there are three sides to every leadership problem. And, if the leader gets this, he will see that every problem is easily solvable." Over the years, the understanding and application of this message became clear to Michael.

All leadership challenges have three sides: the leader, opportunities/problems, and the resources to address them.

You need to explain: why are specific goals important? The goals are not *my* goals, they are *our* goals. Leaders can't just say, "because I said so."

Jacquelin Holzman

—————————————————————

Leadership is driven by our sense of curiosity: what's out there, what's the next challenge? Link that with a desire to help others to make things better, and voila!

Shannon Tessier

—————————————————————

You can't start off with forty-five priorities!! Your staff will write you off right away! Clarity is important; reasoning is important!

Not knowing where you want to go, too many targets, too many things to do, too much confusion cannot be good for your team.

Jacquelin Holzman

—————————————————————

When it's decision time, make sure you have the best facts on the problem that you can find. That doesn't mean delay, delay, delay, but take what you can get and then move on.

Jean Boyle

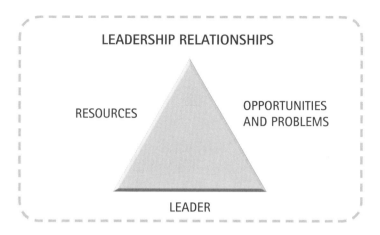

A leader needs to recognize and understand that a problem is real or that the opportunities are there. She needs to have the experience to translate what she sees and communicate that reality to the resources that will take action. This is why they are there!

Communicating the reality requires both the leader and the followers to engage in what we call a leadership conversation. These conversations are two-way, in that they temporarily set aside hierarchical relationships. They are explorative. They stretch to allow each participant to offer and receive information and ideas. Finally, these conversations must be "safe." All must feel free to speak up. Everyone's ideas are required to derive the best solutions.

In the end, everyone involved will return to their roles and appropriate responsibilities within the hierarchy – until the next leadership conversation. The end result is a clear understanding by everyone of how they will apply their individual MVPs within the context of individual and organizational priorities. They will be "on the same page."

The resources (team, followers, workers, plus their equipment, time, funding, etc.) need to understand their level of commitment and need to be trained, equipped, and motivated to derive and then present appropriate solutions and actions.

This may be connected to lessons learned in "Management 101." Efficient, logical, and purposeful, just using the management model will deliver results. But we want high performance. This requires the overlay of a *Leadership Cultural Framework*.

I don't mind doing your job, but if I'm doing your job, then
what are you doing? And who is doing my job?

Jan Kaminski

What happens in the dynamic with employees that causes them to
want to perform at a high level? In my opinion, the following:

Leadership — following a leader with a vision they
understand and values they believe in

Recognition — of what they have done or are doing

Respect — professional and personal

Community — being part of a team working toward the same end

Reward — e.g., assignments, tools, money — usually last
on the dynamic list

Deborah Dickson

Often the leader has to pause and make sure that followers
understand more than just the passion for an idea. They
need to have a practical plan to get there, too!

Shannon Tessier

A leader can demonstrate the values, promote the vision, and can
even hold employees' hands from time to time. Employees need to
understand that their responsibility is to take the initiative, to do the
right things, on their own, for the right reasons, just as the leader would.

Rosemarie Leclair

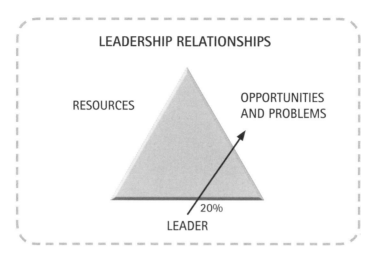

When we talked about twenty-first-century context, we presented the view that leaders must spend 20 percent of their time looking to the future strategic conditions and 80 percent of their effort on operations and transactional commitments. Above is the representation of that 20 percent.

It takes a great deal of discipline for a leader to ensure that sufficient time is spent looking over the horizon when the day-to-day challenges are often overwhelming. However, this is a mandatory function. Leaders must make this commitment to their teams so that there are no surprises (or at least not too many).

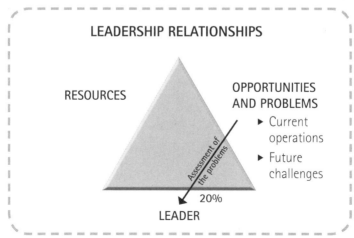

An additional component of this 20 percent are the conclusions the leader draws from the situations and strategic context

Good leaders identify the priorities and make the tough decisions to stay on the correct course. This isn't about what's right or wrong, but rather what you need to focus on.

Roger Greenberg

A large part of leadership is knowing what your goals and objectives are. And then how you are going to do it. I must be honest, sometimes I've been afraid to death. But I wouldn't give the appearance of being frightened to death because it was something I wanted to do.

John Watts

You have a group of people who like you, trust you, believe in you. You've told them where they are going, but nothing is that smooth or simple. There are hills and valleys. I've had to lay people off, change the plans, a whole bunch of things that have been very difficult, but they had to be done to protect the greater good.

Jim Durrell

If you are proactive in looking over the horizon and trusting your intuition, you will be able to unbundle the ambiguity, identify potential threats, and find ways to address them.

Jim Orban

he sees ahead. It is particularly important during this reflection phase that the leader "knows what he knows and doesn't know." This is a time to use all your available tools – your knowledge and experience, your peers', your boss's, your subordinates', your coalition's. Your goal is to make the best possible interpretation from the best possible assessment.

The next component of the model requires that the leader provide to the available resources a translated version of the opportunity and problem assessment. This translation has to accommodate all levels of sophistication and an understanding of the capacity of the resources available. This translation is part of the leadership conversation we spoke about earlier.

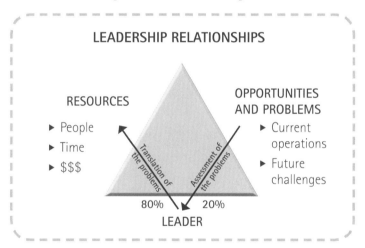

In addition to understanding the challenges, the leader needs to include in the translation the expected results, including scope, timing, funding, quality, and so forth.

It is important to note that in almost all cases that we have researched, the successful leader does not provide "the how" unless absolutely required. At this stage of things, the "why" is much more important.

There are all kinds of positive implications to withholding solutions. Leaders send a message of trust and permission when they resist providing "the how." They guarantee resource ownership of solutions selected and they guarantee team growth and confidence. This is a "teaching them how to fish" moment.

I believe that one has to conquer the basics of what one does and then be allowed to freely explore the possibility of what might be. That would be a workplace of value!

Gerry Arial

— — — — — — — — — — — — — — — — —

Everybody needs to know where they stand. Boundaries need to be drawn around the agreed limits of the employees' discretion and authority.

Rob Lindsay

— — — — — — — — — — — — — — — — —

Give your team members some room to grow, to problem-solve on their own; trust them. Simply put, your leadership job is really to create the right conditions for others to grow.

Shannon Tessier

— — — — — — — — — — — — — — — — —

Keep your team on the same page. People often hear what they want to hear and not what you said. Wrap things up; pull your direct reports to the same point that puts everyone on the same wavelength. Clarify roles, tasks, and the message that is being taken to others. You'll get one shot at this for each new challenge. Make it right.

Rosemarie Leclair

— — — — — — — — — — — — — — — — —

There is a huge difference between delegation and abdication. You delegate to the skills of your team. Abdication . . . that's something else entirely. If you don't know the difference, you will be in a lot of trouble, and soon!

Jim Durrell

The real action phase in the relationship belongs to the resource team. They take their understanding of the leader's translation, reorganize their resources and priorities, and move to find the best solution for the moment they face.

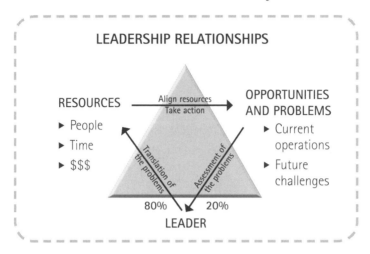

So far, all we have talked about is a one-dimensional movement of information from the opportunities and problems to the leader, to the resources, to the solutions. But in fact there are direct and parallel interactions going on almost all the time – more leadership conversations!

Not only do leaders interpret and transmit challenges, they listen for the echo of consequences across the spectrum of activities. These communication linkages are complex and critical to the success of leaders and followers being able to stay on the same page at the same time.

We will discuss this aspect in the leadership themes following in Section 3, "Know What You Know/Know What You Don't Know," Leadership Assessment #4, "Coaching Others and Collaboration."

In a final phase of this model, in the next figure, we show the residual elements. No high-performance team can blindly pursue solutions without cross-checking to make sure the conditions for success are present. Just as the leader does, the resources need to spend time assessing the problems and opportunities facing them. Their assessment will be at a more tactical level, and must not be omitted or ignored.

Employees with real potential often react best when the leader just poses the problem, letting the solutions flow from the employees' capacity and experience.

Rob Lindsay

--- --- --- --- --- --- --- --- --- --- --- --- --- --- ---

If I left the CEO position, I believe the organization would continue to behave along the same lines of value and vision that I have tried to instill. In part, this is because my job has been to build a platform, then adjust my role to deal less and less in those things that are the variable component of work. This includes quality management, employment equity, environmental sustainability, and other things that are value-based. I would leave behind a platform with structural support that is self-sustainable and that is based on fundamental corporate values.

Franklin Holtforster

--- --- --- --- --- --- --- --- --- --- --- --- --- --- ---

If you think that you can make change happen through one leader, think again. Each level of employee has a contribution to make, and the leader has to make sure that happens. Perhaps all that middle managers should do is make that happen above all else. Every player has to know why things are happening.

Jacquelin Holzman

--- --- --- --- --- --- --- --- --- --- --- --- --- --- ---

Leading is not about giving the orders. It is about providing a clear vision and about giving employees the power they need to get things done.

Jean Boyle

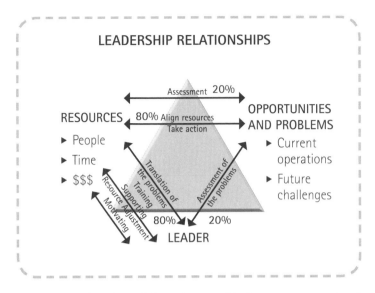

Also in the final model we have added some transmittal and receipt activities for the leader. These activities are related to optimizing resource capacity. This could be adding, subtracting, reorienting, redesigning, retraining, or motivating resources. Basically, the leader is uniformly and resolutely applying Leadership Rules #1 and #2. Rule #3 is used to promote confidence and to provide a forum for adjustment.

So here we have a completed model, and even if that were all you did, you would be able to take on new challenges, embrace new opportunities, and maintain effectiveness. To move to the high-performance applied leadership level, there is one more critical element to add — the Leadership Cultural Framework.

Leadership Cultural Framework

Vision, values, and behaviours are the heart and engine of the high-performance applied leadership team. When combined, they provide the unifying power of a Leadership Cultural Framework. When this framework exists and all team members operate within it, the capacity of the team far exceeds what science would have predicted.

This framework is a central factor and provides individuals and the team as a whole with a context within which the team can operate with confidence and mutual trust in the leadership

Make your organization "change ready." You need them to focus on where they need to be taking the company, not their day-to-day paycheque.

Rosemarie Leclair

I watch what we do and stand up for the best we can do, whatever that is. In the time I have available, I make sure I contribute to the situations, organizations, and issues where I can make a real and positive difference. If it is only for the glory or the social networking, forget it; time is too precious for that.

Roger Greenberg

In order that followers follow "smartly," they need the leader to give them the right kind of information, the information they need for their particular function. The broader the function, the more info required.

Jim Durrell

Maybe there are cleaner, less messy ways to get from here to there, but none that build real teamwork as well.

Rob Lindsay

We are all on the same page with communications and goals. Truth and candor first; we won't sugar-coat the reality.

Jim Orban

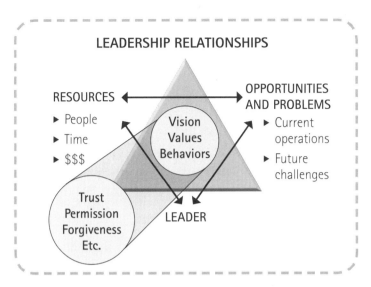

conversation and action modes. When this framework is in place, and the leader and the team are working within it, an extraordinary capacity is built: The power of the team is harnessed and the potential for meeting every challenge is in place.

Creating a Leadership Cultural Framework

You can develop a Leadership Cultural Framework in a fairly straightforward manner, using a normal and accepted change management process.

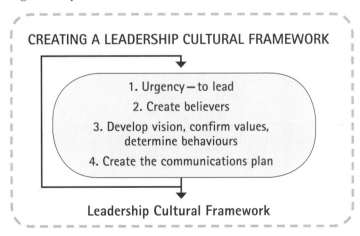

If you and your team truly intend to adopt a high-performance leadership-based approach, you need to first confirm

In hard times especially, every employee understands what's happening. The leader's role is to encourage realism and get everyone on the same page; but at the same time, the leader doesn't have to go looking for trouble. The employees know the score; they know that the leader's door is open. If there is something troubling you, come and see me. We'll sort it out.

Jim Durrell

— — — — — — — — — — — — — — — — — —

When we have a crisis at work, deadlines, lots of priorities, and so on, I pull the team together and make sure we are all on the same page. I set goals that are achievable without compromising quality. Individuals can then organize their efforts, stay creative, and make things right. Those are my priorities.

Gerry Arial

— — — — — — — — — — — — — — — — — —

Sometimes my experience leads me to see the danger in letting the really strong employee rush off in a wrong direction. My challenge is to keep the good ones motivated and energized, while also keeping the negativity and damage from overenthusiastic effort to a minimum.

Rob Lindsay

— — — — — — — — — — — — — — — — — —

Someone once said the best way to get a sense of the culture of an organization is to understand what people are saying and doing when you are not looking or listening.

Jim Orban

that you are all feeling the same level of urgency. This agreement leads to the establishment of a believer group that become the champions of the change.

The believer group must then establish safe and open communication mechanisms, set aside personal agendas and prejudices, and look past personal gain in favour of team and organizational success. This is the second critical step, and often a challenge to achieve. The believer group's success and resulting confidence will provide the ignition source for the total change. Without believer group success, it is not possible to successfully complete and deploy the Leadership Cultural Framework.

The third step involves the complete team in facilitated and structured discussion to ensure that everyone has a chance to contribute to, understand, and ultimately agree to the core elements of the Leadership Cultural Framework. These discussions begin with the leader's presentation of the strategic intention for the team and the organization. They conclude with everyone having contributed to the value structure and behaviour expectations that will govern everyone and will permit everyone to seek and operate at their MVP.

"FAILURE IS NOT AN OPTION."

Without urgency, you cannot create enough momentum to make the change possible. Without a believer group, you cannot grow the necessary commitment. Without a vision, you will have no direction, no target to hit.

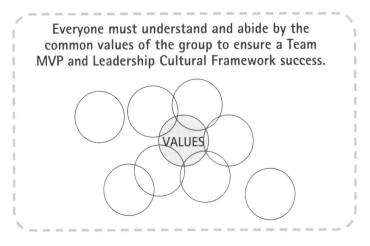

Everyone must understand and abide by the common values of the group to ensure a Team MVP and Leadership Cultural Framework success.

When looking for new employees, look for character and value first. The best employees will want to do things for the right reasons.

Rob Lindsay

- - - - - - - - - - - - - - - - - -

It is okay to ask for support and advice. You need to rely on others to help you expand the realm of possible solutions. Having a network for leaders is important for these kinds of situations and for regular business. You need to bounce ideas off others.

France Jacovella

- - - - - - - - - - - - - - - - - -

When we hire, we look first at attributes, character, and value; then at community involvement; and then at skills and the "tech" things. Am I being clear about where our priorities are?

J-P Soublière

- - - - - - - - - - - - - - - - - -

You must make sure that you have the right person, the right resources for him, and the right training; that the work environment helps him to get things done. Give him goals and give him a system, standards, and power to make decisions on his own.

Jacquelin Holzman

- - - - - - - - - - - - - - - - - -

Leadership qualities must include the ability to communicate at a very high level. You simply must be able to get the messages out while conveying your passion, your vision, your sense of enthusiasm and optimism. Your followers really want to be excited and involved in whatever task you need them to do. Your approach must create the desire in them.

Shannon Tessier

Without a common set of values and behaviours and a commitment to those values and behaviours across the entire organization, you will most certainly fail. Even if you have a common set of values and behaviours and a commitment to them, failure is certain when they are poorly transmitted or misinterpreted, or when violators of value are not held accountable.

The diagram on the previous page represents a team that is held together by values. Some values overlap. Some are disconnected. Team members who refuse to be connected on values can contribute and can be managed, but will not rise to the team's MVP level.

When things go wrong, it is often attributable to values gone wrong. Either the values were not clear or they were really not agreed to. Actions that violate the agreed-upon values by individuals – leader or followers – can threaten the Leadership Cultural Framework. Once values are violated, it is very difficult to reformulate them. Credibility has been lost.

WEHN TINHGS GO WRNOG!

- ▶ Competing values
- ▶ Value misinterpretation
- ▶ Actions that appear to threaten values
- ▶ A safe place to talk

The last but not the least important issue is the requirement of the leader to develop and nurture opportunities for every team member to speak safely about anything with the full confidence that these conversations are protected and correctly interpreted. Without the opportunity for frank and open discussion in private, the leader will have failed to build a level of trust that will withstand the inevitable pressures and adjustments that the twenty-first-century turbulence creates.

The final step in the Leadership Cultural Framework process is communication – planning and execution. The communication plan must address the needs of all levels of the organization. It must promote and reinforce the vision, values, and behaviour agreement. It must lay out the strategic context

It always seems to come back to values and principles. How you stick to them provides predictability for others. They will learn quickly where you will go, and they'll be able to get there first. At the same time, they will be pretty confident that they are on the right track, even when the leader is not there.

Rosemarie Leclair

— — — — — — — — — — — — — — — — — —

Trust in one's subordinates is everything, and it starts with recruiting for the right values and skill sets.

Jean Boyle

— — — — — — — — — — — — — — — — — —

I hired people if I thought they would work well as part of the group. If they didn't have the same beliefs when they came in, they had to want to change or to contribute to changing it.

Dave Dickson

— — — — — — — — — — — — — — — — — —

Senior leaders must move beyond the talk and get to the walking part. When we were developing a vision and mission statement, I looked at some statements prepared from other companies, and one in particular stood out and I loved it! I said, "Let's just use those words, they are great!" It turned out that these were from ENRON! So much for using that statement of value!

Roger Greenberg

and expectations of the leader. And it must include the predetermined safety mechanisms that will promote open and frank communication amongst all levels.

We have provided the strategic level steps in a sample plan below, demonstrating the implementation of a Leadership Cultural Framework within an organization.

Create a communication plan that fits your organization. As long as you have gone through the development process correctly, you will find that the Leadership Cultural Framework is very resilient and will support any number of organizational scenarios.

Monitor and evaluate

The Leadership Cultural Framework requires monitoring and evaluation. On a regular basis, you should subject it to a critical validation process. As a minimum, ask the questions shown in the following diagram, "Validating Your Leadership Cultural Framework." The answers will help guide the continuous improvement of the framework and, just as important, will keep every team member committed to its fulfillment.

On an annual basis, for example, (prior to your strategic planning session), review your Leadership Cultural Framework and refresh it, as a group. This is a worthwhile and easily scheduled exercise that will provide an excellent foundation for the strategic discussions that follow.

Personal integrity is an important element of leadership, but you have to earn it. People have to trust you. They do that by watching you and how you act, over time. If people trust you, then you will be successful. I don't think you are going to find a real true leader who isn't trustworthy.

John Watts

People understand . . . If you are doing things to line your pockets . . . they understand. If you are doing the right things for the right reasons, they understand. If you build relationships, people will trust you and will trust you to make even the toughest decisions, even the ones that will directly affect them in some way. They'll understand it.

Jim Durrell

Most good leaders don't allow the culture to form them — they form the culture required.

Jim Orban

There is nothing more disappointing to me than to see those whom I have trusted and worked with betray my confidence in them by not living up to their potential and, more critically, to their professed values. If it turns out that I know nothing or very little about applied leadership, it won't hurt my feelings but it will definitely pique my curiosity.

Gerry Arial

When we get it right, it gets out by word of mouth to those outside the organization: that is, what we are trying to do, our philosophy and work ethic.

Rob Lindsay

Finding your leadership "centre" — conclusions

VALIDATING YOUR
LEADERSHIP CULTURAL FRAMEWORK

Everyone must be able to answer these questions:

▶ What is included and does it work?

▶ How is it integrated into the management processes and leadership style?

▶ Does it exist at all levels? If not, why not?

▶ How do you talk about it and use it?

▶ Is it safe to talk about it?

▶ Who is the keeper?

▶ Who is the inspirational source?

▶ How is it kept alive? Is there a feedback loop?

▶ How is it measured?

From developing individual understanding of the Maximum Value Proposition, leadership energy management, and the steps to build team performance, we have tried to provide a simple and easily understood recipe that will lead to higher performance for you and your team. Using what we call "Management 101" and overlaying a Leadership Cultural Framework, you and your team can raise your game significantly.

Leadership can be messy. It is an art, after all. There will be mistakes made, detours taken, and dead ends pursued. Count on it. You can also count on team behaviour that will recover from mistakes, find the right path, and achieve your intended goals. There are bound to be moments of doubt but there will also be moments of absolute certainty and relief that you chose leadership over management.

What follows is a Leadership Cultural Framework summary checklist for you and your team. This is something that you can deploy prior to your strategic planning session or use in a less formal way on a regular basis.

In the short term, leadership can be messy.
Rob Lindsay

There are things that I don't know that I don't know.
You must genuinely listen to others, to discover things
that you did not know that you did not know.
France Jacovella

As a leader you don't have to be right all the time. If you take
this attitude, it excludes you from learning and stops information
from flowing up to you. It also stops you from teaching others.
Franklin Holtforster

If someone calls the mayor to say, "There is a rabbit drowning in
my swimming pool," what am I to do? I suppose we could try to
teach it to swim! You might have to get a scoop or something.
Seriously, your staff needs to have the confidence
and power to get on with things.
Jacquelin Holzman

Listening is probably one of the most important characteristics
that an individual needs to develop in order to become an
effective leader. Listening — *not* delivery, *not* talking — listening.
Jean Boyle

LEADERSHIP CULTURAL FRAMEWORK
SUMMARY CHECKLIST

FRAMEWORK:

▸ **Leadership urgency**

Why us? Why now?

▸ **What do we want to accomplish in the end? What it could be?**

What would be included?

Would it be integrated into our management processes and leadership style?

Would it exist at all levels? If not, who would get it?

Who would be the inspirational source?

Who would be the keeper?

▸ **Leadership vision, values, and behaviour rules**

What are they?

LEADERSHIP COMMUNICATION PLAN:

How do we make sure that our Leadership Cultural Framework is cascaded to the organization?

How and when do we talk about it and use it?

MONITORING AND EVALUATION:

How will our leadership framework be deployed?

How will it be kept alive?

How will we know we are leading better?

Will there be feedback loops (informal and formal performance indicators)?

Two lists are provided in the appendices that will help you with Applied Leadership Basics: the Leadership Cultural Framework Checklist (Appendix A) and the "Kaminski List" (Appendix B).

Adjust them to your specific needs and keep both of these lists at hand. Check them at least once a month to ensure that you are adhering to *your* Leadership Cultural Framework.

One of the things I try to instill is that everyone is the CEO of their area. The receptionist is the CEO of reception. The sales rep is the CEO of a territory. The guy doing the packaging and shipping is the CEO of that area.

Jan Kaminski

Sometimes even the most passionate and talented of employees lose their way, almost as if they are suddenly and inexplicably lost.

Shannon Tessier

Knowing who is valued is wasted knowledge unless you also tell them that they are valued and then invest in them.

Rosemarie Leclair

One learns from these things how to motivate people. My style is quiet and I have a tendency to under-celebrate somewhat. I try harder these days.

Roger Greenberg

Tell a poor performer to start looking for a job and do not embarrass him. Give him the time to look. He will know he has not performed. Trust has to be there to make this happen and work.

Dave Dickson

To conclude this section, we have brought together the three basic Leadership Rules:

LEADERSHIP BY THE NUMBERS . . .

LEADERSHIP RULE #1:
I promise to make you better, *and*
you promise to do your part.

LEADERSHIP RULE #2:
I want you to promise to hold me to promise #1, *and*
I will hold you to your promise to do your part.

LEADERSHIP RULE #3:
I promise to celebrate our successes in public, *and*
discuss our failures in private and I ask you to do the same.

Leadership conversations are framed by these basic rules and by the shared vision, values, and behaviours that are at the centre of the applied leadership model. It is a leader's role to continually inspire, energize, and monitor the level of effort (team and individual) and the results of that effort. Because of the rates of change we are experiencing, leaders are challenged with continually adjusting the direction, speed, and resources used. The leader's goal is to not only keep performance aligned with evolving expectations, but to get to this finish line with everyone she started with. Still following; still leading; still engaged!

KWYK/KWYDK

(Know What You Know / Know What You Don't Know)

Right from the beginning, the leaders with whom we conducted our conversations revealed their perspective that leaders do not have to know everything, but they do have to know what they know and what they don't know. Their leadership credibility depends on this awareness.

Thinking about this is a bit like *Back to the Future* or *Alice and the Looking Glass* — a little mind-bending. How do we know what we don't know? How do we know what we know?

Looking at ourselves honestly, critically, and thoroughly requires some courage and the ability to stand outside of ourselves, accepting our knowledge and capacities without being judgmental, critical, or falsely modest. We must be honest with ourselves. We must reach a conclusion about our situational knowledge areas and develop the confidence to use what we know or ask for help with those areas where we lack knowledge. Leadership, after all, is a team game, not an individual sport.

In order to help you assess yourself against typical leadership competencies, we have developed two tools: a KWYK/ KWYDK tool and a Leadership Self-Assessment tool. These self-assessment tools are intended to stimulate your curiosity, build your self awareness, and create the opportunity for you to optimize your strengths so that you can make the best possible contribution to your team.

KWYK/KWYDK Knowledge Grid tool
— for the individual and for the team

The Knowledge Grid helps to determine what you know and don't know about yourself; *and* what you think your team knows and doesn't know about itself. There are ten key leadership competencies for your knowledge review:

1. *Strategic thinking.* Are you a big-picture person or do you prefer the details? Are you more interested in developing a plan or following it?

2. *Self-confidence.* Do you believe in yourself and your team?

3. *Ethics and integrity.* As a key part of the vision, values, and behaviour agreement among team members, do you understand and strive to adhere to your and your team's true north?

4. *Creativity and innovation.* Are you fulfilling your and your team's need to be creative and innovative? Do you have safe conversations that invite all ideas? Do you brainstorm to find the best possible solutions?

5. *Flexibility and adaptability.* Have you developed a comfort level with change? Or do you prefer the predictable?

6. *Ability to inspire vision.* Do you understand the requirement to inspire yourself and others to the highest possible vision of the future? Do you think about the consequences of being stuck in the present?

7. *Communication and information.* Do you and your team hide from each other or hide information? Do you and your team understand the power of dialogue?

8. *Building relationships.* Do you limit your relationships? Are you engaging everyone?

9. *Teamwork:* Are you a team of one or do you use the power of the group?

10. *Management and empowerment.* Do you understand and apply Leadership Rule #1? Do you create opportunities to bring everyone to a higher level?

There are two sections for each competency. The first refers to you and you alone. The second refers to "My Team" — that is, the team you work with on a day-to-day basis or the team of which you are a member.

Take the following test and see where you fall on the "know what you know and what you don't know" grid. Please select the answers that most candidly reflect your observations about yourself and your team. This exercise will help you to identify real strengths and opportunities for improvement.

1. *Strategic Thinking*

For each item below, **circle** a rating on the scoring grid that most accurately matches your agreement/disagreement with the statement.

	Competency — Strategic Thinking	STRONGLY DISAGREE	DISAGREE	NEUTRAL	AGREE	STRONGLY AGREE
ME						
1	I am able to look at the big picture.	1	2	3	4	5
2	I tend to focus on the specific tasks at hand.	5	4	3	2	1
3	My conceptual vision is my target.	1	2	3	4	5
4	Strategic thinking is for planners.	5	4	3	2	1
5	I enjoy strategic planning and keep it in mind.	1	2	3	4	5
6	I can do annual planning but it does not change the day-to-day.	5	4	3	2	1
MY TEAM						
7	We develop and regularly revisit the strategy.	1	2	3	4	5
8	We know there must be a strategy but we can't figure out what it is or why it is needed.	5	4	3	2	1
9	We are aware of the overall organizational strategy and try to connect to it.	1	2	3	4	5
10	Strategic plans are for MBAs.	5	4	3	2	1
11	We are actively involved in creating and living the strategy.	1	2	3	4	5
12	We will follow strategy, but the daily crises overtake it.	5	4	3	2	1
	Add the circled scores and enter the sum in the box below					

The Strategic Thinking score means I/my team has:

60–46 Advanced capability	30–16 Opportunities for growth
45–31 Working capability	15–01 Critical need to improve

Key findings:

What do I think are the strengths of my/my team's **strategic thinking** skills?

1 _____

_____

2 _____

_____

3 _____

_____

What could I do to improve my/my team's **strategic thinking**?

1 _____

_____

2 _____

_____

3 _____

_____

2.   Self-Confidence

For each item below, **circle** a rating on the scoring grid that most accurately matches your agreement/disagreement with the statement.

	Competency— Self-Confidence	STRONGLY DISAGREE	DISAGREE	NEUTRAL	AGREE	STRONGLY AGREE
	ME					
1	I understand my strengths and limitations.	1	2	3	4	5
2	I'm really not sure about my ability to cope.	5	4	3	2	1
3	Most of the time I can step up to the task.	1	2	3	4	5
4	Uncertainty is my normal feeling.	5	4	3	2	1
5	I don't mind making mistakes; I'll try to get it better the next time.	1	2	3	4	5
6	Ethics and integrity are not a high priority.	5	4	3	2	1
	MY TEAM					
7	Our team is really together and we can get things done.	1	2	3	4	5
8	We have really strong players who tend to overtake the others.	5	4	3	2	1
9	Depending on the challenge, we can be effective.	1	2	3	4	5
10	I'm not sure our team believes in itself.	5	4	3	2	1
11	We are unanimous in our sense of confidence, no matter what!	1	2	3	4	5
12	When there are challenges, someone may step up.	5	4	3	2	1
	Add the circled scores and enter the sum in the box below					

The Self-Confidence score means I/my team has:

60–46 Advanced capability	30–16 Opportunities for growth
45–31 Working capability	15–01 Critical need to improve

Key findings:

What are the leadership self-confidence components for my team and me?

1 _____

_____

2 _____

_____

3 _____

_____

What could I/we do to better understand or more effectively improve my/our leadership self-confidence?

1 _____

_____

2 _____

_____

3 _____

_____

3.   Ethics and Integrity

For each item below, **circle** a rating on the scoring grid that most accurately matches your agreement/disagreement with the statement.

	Competency — Ethics and Integrity	STRONGLY DISAGREE	DISAGREE	NEUTRAL	AGREE	STRONGLY AGREE
	ME					
1	I believe in and show my integrity every day.	1	2	3	4	5
2	I sometimes bend my own rules.	5	4	3	2	1
3	I'll bend but not break the standards.	1	2	3	4	5
4	The only rule is to survive.	5	4	3	2	1
5	I don't waver from my beliefs.	1	2	3	4	5
6	Ethics and integrity are not a high priority.	5	4	3	2	1
	MY TEAM					
7	We demonstrate honesty and forthrightness.	1	2	3	4	5
8	We do whatever is necessary to get the job done.	5	4	3	2	1
9	Most of the time, we support our agreed-upon values.	1	2	3	4	5
10	We don't walk the talk.	5	4	3	2	1
11	We don't sacrifice our team ethics for convenience or wins.	1	2	3	4	5
12	We don't always keep our values in sight.	5	4	3	2	1
	Add the circled scores and enter the sum in the box below					

The Ethics and Integrity score means I/my team has:

60–46 Advanced capability	30–16 Opportunities for growth
45–31 Working capability	15–01 Critical need to improve

Key findings:

What are the leadership ethics and integrity components for my team and me?

1 _____

_____

2 _____

_____

3 _____

_____

What could I/we do to better understand or more effectively improve my/our leadership ethics and integrity?

1 _____

_____

2 _____

_____

3 _____

_____

4. *Creativity and Innovation*

For each item below, **circle** a rating on the scoring grid that most accurately matches your agreement/disagreement with the statement.

Competency— Creativity and Innovation	STRONGLY DISAGREE	DISAGREE	NEUTRAL	AGREE	STRONGLY AGREE
ME					
1	I love the idea of brainstorming new concepts and ideas.	1	2	3	4	5
2	These are things I'd rather do last.	5	4	3	2	1
3	Fresh and unusual ideas are my forte.	1	2	3	4	5
4	Innovation and inspiration are not required for my work.	5	4	3	2	1
5	Sometimes I can really find creative and innovative solutions.	1	2	3	4	5
6	I think that new approaches should be adopted, if at all, slowly and carefully.	5	4	3	2	1
MY TEAM					
7	We get together regularly to brainstorm and help each other with creative ideas.	1	2	3	4	5
8	Except for a few of us, creativity and innovation are rare and are really not required.	5	4	3	2	1
9	We can usually create innovative solutions to our problems.	1	2	3	4	5
10	This team does not need to be creative. We like the processes we have.	5	4	3	2	1
11	We like to create and constantly innovate. It keeps us sharp.	1	2	3	4	5
12	Only when the team is in trouble, or under the gun, can we find a solution.	5	4	3	2	1
	Add the circled scores and enter the sum in the box below					

The Creativity and Innovation score means I/my team has:

60–46 Advanced capability	30–16 Opportunities for growth
45–31 Working capability	15–01 Critical need to improve

Key findings:

What are the creativity and innovation components for my team and me?

1 _____

_____

2 _____

_____

3 _____

_____

What could I/we do to better understand or more effectively improve my/our creativity and innovation?

1 _____

_____

2 _____

_____

3 _____

_____

5. *Flexibility and Adaptability*

For each item below, **circle** a rating on the scoring grid that most accurately matches your agreement/disagreement with the statement.

	Competency — Flexibility and Adaptability	STRONGLY DISAGREE	DISAGREE	NEUTRAL	AGREE	STRONGLY AGREE
	ME					
1	I love to juggle all the priorities and to get things done.	1	2	3	4	5
2	I really don't like to alter course unnecessarily.	5	4	3	2	1
3	Changes of pace and prioritizing are refreshing.	1	2	3	4	5
4	I'd really like my work to stay predictable.	5	4	3	2	1
5	When things require changing, I find the day exciting.	1	2	3	4	5
6	I don't mind some changes but not too many to interfere with my regular workload.	5	4	3	2	1
	MY TEAM					
7	We all can easily adjust to just about anything.	1	2	3	4	5
8	We're pretty fixed in our methods and routines.	5	4	3	2	1
9	Most of the time, the team adapts to change.	1	2	3	4	5
10	This team does not react well to challenge or change.	5	4	3	2	1
11	Change is expected and we handle it well.	1	2	3	4	5
12	We prefer to maintain our current ways of doing things.	5	4	3	2	1
	Add the circled scores and enter the sum in the box below					

The Flexibility and Adaptability score means I/my team has:

60–46 Advanced capability	30–16 Opportunities for growth
45–31 Working capability	15–01 Critical need to improve

Key findings:

What are the flexibility and adaptability components for my team and me?

1 _____

_____

2 _____

_____

3 _____

_____

What could I/we do to better understand or more effectively improve my/our flexibility and adaptability?

1 _____

_____

2 _____

_____

3 _____

_____

6. Inspire Vision

For each item below, **circle** a rating on the scoring grid that most accurately matches your agreement/disagreement with the statement.

	Competency— Inspire Vision	STRONGLY DISAGREE	DISAGREE	NEUTRAL	AGREE	STRONGLY AGREE
	ME					
1	I truly want to inspire others.	1	2	3	4	5
2	It's not something I do.	5	4	3	2	1
3	When we seem to be boxed in, I try to get others to think out of the box.	1	2	3	4	5
4	Even if I had a vision, I wouldn't know how to communicate it.	5	4	3	2	1
5	I remind others of our vision and inspire them to reach for it.	1	2	3	4	5
6	Mostly, I rely on the vision of others (e.g., my boss).	5	4	3	2	1
	MY TEAM					
7	On this team, we try to inspire each other.	1	2	3	4	5
8	It's not something our team does with great success.	5	4	3	2	1
9	Our team relies on the agreed-upon vision. It keeps us focused.	1	2	3	4	5
10	"Visioning" is never done on this team.	5	4	3	2	1
11	We know what it is and we are striving to attain it.	1	2	3	4	5
12	Our vision is the day's workload.	5	4	3	2	1
	Add the circled scores and enter the sum in the box below					

The Inspire Vision score means I/my team has:

60–46 Advanced capability	30–16 Opportunities for growth
45–31 Working capability	15–01 Critical need to improve

Key findings:

What are the inspire vision components for my team and me?

1 _____

_____

2 _____

_____

3 _____

_____

What could I/we do to better understand or more effectively improve my/our skills to inspire vision?

1 _____

_____

2 _____

_____

3 _____

_____

7. *Communicate and Inform*

For each item below, **circle** a rating on the scoring grid that most accurately matches your agreement/disagreement with the statement.

	Competency— Communicate and Inform	STRONGLY DISAGREE	DISAGREE	NEUTRAL	AGREE	STRONGLY AGREE
	ME					
1	I am always sharing, asking, and listening.	1	2	3	4	5
2	I find it hard to be open and transparent.	5	4	3	2	1
3	I take time to share and listen.	1	2	3	4	5
4	I don't find the time or opportunity to communicate and connect with others.	5	4	3	2	1
5	I communicate whether it's required or not.	1	2	3	4	5
6	When there is a meeting, I can participate – if I'm asked a question.	5	4	3	2	1
	MY TEAM					
7	We understand the importance of open communication and we listen to each other.	1	2	3	4	5
8	We rarely share information except when we are complaining or going down memory lane.	5	4	3	2	1
9	We are a transparent and sharing group.	1	2	3	4	5
10	We get together. We take minutes. But that is as far as the communication goes.	5	4	3	2	1
11	We can communicate openly and transparently across the organization – not just within our team.	1	2	3	4	5
12	Sometimes we keep information to ourselves.	5	4	3	2	1
	Add the circled scores and enter the sum in the box below					

The Communicate and Inform score means I/my team has:

60–46 Advanced capability	30–16 Opportunities for growth
45–31 Working capability	15–01 Critical need to improve

Key findings:

What are the communicate and inform components for my team and me?

1 _____

_____

2 _____

_____

3 _____

_____

What could I/we do to better understand or more effectively improve my/our skills to communicate and inform?

1 _____

_____

2 _____

_____

3 _____

_____

8.   *Build Relationships*

For each item below, **circle** a rating on the scoring grid that most accurately matches your agreement/disagreement with the statement.

	Competency— Build Relationships	STRONGLY DISAGREE	DISAGREE	NEUTRAL	AGREE	STRONGLY AGREE
	ME					
1	I get along with everyone.	1	2	3	4	5
2	I keep my interpersonal relations outside of work.	5	4	3	2	1
3	I let all my colleagues get near me.	1	2	3	4	5
4	I don't relate well to others.	5	4	3	2	1
5	I don't put up fences and I like to be included.	1	2	3	4	5
6	I have only a few people that I will reach out to.	5	4	3	2	1
	MY TEAM					
7	We make sure that every member feels welcomed and valued.	1	2	3	4	5
8	We sometimes forget to be inclusive.	5	4	3	2	1
9	We do not have cliques and elitists on our team.	1	2	3	4	5
10	We don't work well together.	5	4	3	2	1
11	We don't permit isolation or exclusivity.	1	2	3	4	5
12	We are only friendly enough to survive.	5	4	3	2	1
	Add the circled scores and enter the sum in the box below					

The Build Relationships score means I/my team has:

60–46 Advanced capability	30–16 Opportunities for growth
45–31 Working capability	15–01 Critical need to improve

Key findings:

What are the build relationships components for my team and me?

1 _____

_____

2 _____

_____

3 _____

_____

What could I/we do to better understand or more effectively improve my/our skills to build relationships?

1 _____

_____

2 _____

_____

3 _____

_____

9. *Teamwork*

For each item below, **circle** a rating on the scoring grid that most accurately matches your agreement/disagreement with the statement.

	Competency— Teamwork	STRONGLY DISAGREE	DISAGREE	NEUTRAL	AGREE	STRONGLY AGREE
	ME					
1	I always try to bring value to the team.	1	2	3	4	5
2	I prefer to work alone.	5	4	3	2	1
3	I want the team to be the best it can be.	1	2	3	4	5
4	I find teamwork uncomfortable.	5	4	3	2	1
5	I am at my best in team settings.	1	2	3	4	5
6	I work well in teams if they meet my expectations.	5	4	3	2	1
	MY TEAM					
7	We are always trying to find the best team approach.	1	2	3	4	5
8	Every man/woman for themselves!	5	4	3	2	1
9	We have team challenges that we discuss and work on together.	1	2	3	4	5
10	We are a team in name only.	5	4	3	2	1
11	We always have each other's back.	1	2	3	4	5
12	In moments of crisis, we can't pull together.	5	4	3	2	1
	Add the circled scores and enter the sum in the box below					

The Teamwork score means I/my team has:

60–46 Advanced capability	30–16 Opportunities for growth
45–31 Working capability	15–01 Critical need to improve

Key findings:

What are the teamwork components for my team and me?

1 _____

_____

2 _____

_____

3 _____

_____

What could I/we do to better understand or more effectively improve my/our skills to enhance teamwork?

1 _____

_____

2 _____

_____

3 _____

_____

10. Manage and Empower

For each item below, **circle** a rating on the scoring grid that most accurately matches your agreement/disagreement with the statement.

	Competency— Manage and Empower	STRONGLY DISAGREE	DISAGREE	NEUTRAL	AGREE	STRONGLY AGREE
	ME					
1	Aligning people and empowering them is my strength.	1	2	3	4	5
2	I assign work by terms of reference and seniority.	5	4	3	2	1
3	I don't play favourites. I assign work and hold staff accountable.	1	2	3	4	5
4	I know who works best and I keep them close to me.	5	4	3	2	1
5	Most of the time I can motivate people to think and to be themselves.	1	2	3	4	5
6	Some people are easier to manage than others. I sometimes avoid challenging employees.	5	4	3	2	1
	MY TEAM					
7	We know our roles and our strengths and support each other.	1	2	3	4	5
8	There are only a few of us who can get things done, and we do.	5	4	3	2	1
9	When work stresses permit, we try to mentor each other.	1	2	3	4	5
10	We keep information and our skill sets separate from each other.	5	4	3	2	1
11	Despite the pressure to achieve results, we bring everyone along together.	1	2	3	4	5
12	We do not give stretch assignments to those who have not proven themselves.	5	4	3	2	1
	Add the circled scores and enter the sum in the box below					

The Manage and Empower score means I/my team has:

60–46 Advanced capability	30–16 Opportunities for growth
45–31 Working capability	15–01 Critical need to improve

Key findings:

What are the manage and empower components for my team and me?

1 _____

_____

2 _____

_____

3 _____

_____

What could I/we do to better understand or more effectively improve my/our skills to manage and empower?

1 _____

_____

2 _____

_____

3 _____

_____

The best leaders stay continuously curious about what might be possible.

Shannon Tessier

— — — — — — — — — — — — — — — — — —

In these times of turbulence and volatility, we need to ramp up our communication with staff. Retreats, newsletters, Internet blogging, and so on are required to keep pace with information change rates. Even though I think we communicate well with employees, every employee survey we undertake says that they want more info, more transparency. I think the information helps the employees to trust our senior management team and the course we have chosen.

Roger Greenberg

— — — — — — — — — — — — — — — — — —

Some people do not see themselves as others see them. An individual in the company — a smart, senior engineer — had a 360° review and some of his peers said he was awful. Some of his team said he was terrible. He read it and he said, "Am I like that?" He just couldn't believe that that's how some people saw him. He did not see himself how others saw him. When he sat and read some of the comments, he actually got quite tearful about it and said, "That's it, I'm changing."

John Watts

— — — — — — — — — — — — — — — — —

Depending on where a business or corporation is in its growth pattern, the leadership skills required will be different. Not all leaders will have the full range of capability to be really effective at that point in time.

Jim Durrell

LEADERSHIP ASSESSMENT

In addition to the KWYK and KWYDK Grid, we have found six advanced themes that successful leaders also use and promote. These are not necessarily the final word in leadership concepts, but mastery of them will lead to higher-performance, longer-term successful teams.

The following sections provide background and information on each theme. A self-assessment tool is embedded for each. This provides you with an opportunity to measure where you stand against our research but, more important, a chance to reflect about your own experience within that theme. These advanced leadership themes are:

1. Self-Knowledge and Authenticity
2. Leadership Value Proposition
3. Vision and Values
4. Coaching Others and Collaboration
5. Building Trust
6. Credibility and Authority

Each theme assessment also provides you with an opportunity to identify steps you might take to raise your game within that leadership theme. Your score in each theme will give you a general indication of your knowledge, skill, and comfort level. When you are finished, look at two results: your combined score, which identifies your performance level, and your individual scores that may indicate your need to work on something, even if your performance level is satisfactory or better.

At the conclusion of the theme assessment tool is a personal leadership goal-setting exercise. We encourage you to complete it and use it as a template for your personal leadership growth. The results of these exercises are also key to developing a personal Leadership Framework.

1. Self-Knowledge and Authenticity

As Popeye said, "I yam what I yam." If there was ever a first principle of applied leadership, this could be it. You must understand who and what you are in order to behave and act

Leaders must remember what it was like not to know.

Franklin Holtforster

— — — — — — — — — — — — — — — —

You know what? Some people just need to think less about themselves;
if they did, they would be simply amazing people and team members.

Shannon Tessier

— — — — — — — — — — — — — — — —

In a company like ours, there is a very skilled technical workforce.
Some of them are scientists. Some of them are great individual
contributors. Some of them are good managers. Some of them are
excellent leaders. Some of them are both. A lot of them are neither.

John Watts

— — — — — — — — — — — — — — — —

We don't need to have the same leadership style throughout
the organization but we have to be on the same page. If not,
you won't be able to keep up when we turn that page.

Jim Durrell

— — — — — — — — — — — — — — — —

Sometimes you learn and are motivated by both good and bad leaders
in life — if you understand why they are good or why they are bad.
You are on the right track if you adopt the good and avoid the bad.

Jim Orban

authentically with yourself, your family, your community, and your workplace.

Because we are always in development (from cradle to grave), it would be inappropriate for us to suggest that we are a fixture, that we came into the world with some preordained leadership design in place or that we will develop to a point and stay that way.

Equally inappropriate, but often stated: "This person was a born leader." It's like the "overnight success" who toiled in the minor leagues or off Broadway until "suddenly" discovered as a real talent. Surely we are the product of at least three major influences:

- ▶ Our genetic gifts from our parents and ancestors
- ▶ The effect of the nurturing circumstances of our youth
- ▶ The effect of our experiences and decisions as adults

Much has been written on this.[5] Smarter people than us have figured this stuff out for us. So let's just accept that it is what it is. There are three factors.

The first two factors influence in good and not so good ways. Let's just say that there is nothing to be done with them now. Accept them. You are what you are. From that point on, you continue to learn and develop your leadership personality. Some people have bigger hills to climb when emerging from the nurturing phase of their lives. The gap between where they are and where they might be in the future may be big or small. Either way the gap needs effort to bridge.

The third factor[6] — those things that influence us as adults — observations of good and bad behaviour, extraordinary successes and accomplishments, total failures, inspirational moments, family tragedies, and so on, somehow combine in a unique way (like snowflakes, there are no two alike) to continually create and recreate who we are, not only as a person, but in the context of this subject, your ever-evolving, authentic leadership self.

---

5   Dr. Peter Jensen, *Igniting the Third Factor* (Rockwood, Ont.: Performance Coaching, Inc., 2008).
6   Ibid.

Even if the last and best idea was yours, it's not necessary
to remind everyone every five seconds that it was.

Shannon Tessier

--- --- --- --- --- --- --- --- --- --- --- --- --- --- --- ---

Do not surround yourself with people like yourself to implement change.
Look for complementary and additional strengths in others, express the
vision, and expect the team to grasp the urgency and own the change.

Jim Orban

--- --- --- --- --- --- --- --- --- --- --- --- --- --- --- ---

I want my team members to understand that I will push them
to stretch themselves to their limit. Sometimes we reach the
limit too soon and they have to move on, but that's okay — they
grew at least a bit. Excellence has a distinct price to pay.

Gerry Arial

--- --- --- --- --- --- --- --- --- --- --- --- --- --- --- ---

"Flip-Flops" and cargo shorts at work or generally sloppy
dress may indicate more than just bad taste.

J-P Soublière

--- --- --- --- --- --- --- --- --- --- --- --- --- --- --- ---

Leadership is definitely not a case of influencing by "sound bite."

Rosemarie Leclair

Now we are here to influence you some more. We are convinced that you can continually refine your authentic leadership self, making it more powerful and effective. To do so assumes that you have a clear understanding of where you are standing at the moment: leadership knowledge, personality knowledge, value knowledge, intentions, education, experiences, personal goals, relationship goals, principles of character, table manners, dress code, personal hygiene, linguistic capacity, interpersonal skills, intelligence, physical attributes, mental health, family values, family status, vices, and so on.

An example of how important even the most superficial aspects can be is referenced in marketing studies where 83 percent of the perceived value of an object is determined in the first seven to ten seconds of observation by someone who has never seen the object before. Applied to people, 83 percent of your perceived value (by someone who has never met you) could be determined by the clothes you wear, your stance, the language you use, your manner of greeting, the firmness of your handshake, the look in your eye, your smile, your scent, your acne, your flip flops, your butt-crack-showing jeans, your tight skirt . . .

Unfair? Maybe. Influential? Definitely. It is the whole person that matters, but the effect of our first impressions cannot be underestimated.

In this section, we are going beyond first impressions and delving into what makes us whole. We will continue to provide related nuggets and other exercises to help you come to some understanding of who you are and where you are at this point in time.

People who are in tune with themselves seem to have a way of deploying their capabilities without annoying us or making us jealous of them. They are at peace. They are fun to work with, easy to follow, and often make great leaders. When we find them, we really want to hold onto them, to understand them and learn from them.

Michael remembers: "When I was in the military, I came to the realization that I could be like them. I was inspired to make myself better. I realized I was underutilizing my strengths and over-utilizing my undeveloped areas. I was self-critical and

I don't think I could walk into a room of people, sit down and listen, and then identify leaders. But I certainly would go out of that room thinking we should keep an eye on these three people.

John Watts

— — — — — — — — — — — — — — — — —

I think that at the instinctive level, most everyone wants to be led. I do, and at the same I consider myself a pretty good leader. I'm always looking for someone to lead me — someone I can confidently follow.

Jim Durrell

— — — — — — — — — — — — — — — —

To achieve a high-performance environment, you don't have to constantly be on people's case. There is no surprise or shock involved. Everyone simply needs to know what is expected and the consequences of both success and failure.

Jim Orban

— — — — — — — — — — — — — — — —

One of the real challenges with good leadership is to criticize properly in a way that leads to both better performance and better feelings. It's an art form for sure, but you'd better have a plan, too.

Rob Lindsay

focused on the wrong things. Instead of trying to use my legitimate strengths, I was compensating by trying to overemphasize the strengths I thought were required, whether I had them or not."

If you confuse authority with authenticity, you may believe that since you have the authority to act, you must. For example, if you are responsible for a mailroom, you might think that you need to know everything about every aspect of the mailroom. Then you might think that you need to take responsibility for every aspect of the mailroom and be authoritative on every aspect. The reality is, of course, that you don't.

The leadership reality is that by understanding your authentic self as opposed to your authoritative self, you can take advantage of your strengths to collaborate, teach, analyze, or use some combination of other strengths to influence your mailroom team to meet their goals. Your leadership goal would be to integrate your team's strengths with your strengths to create a result greater than your authority alone could create. Together, the team will *know* more about every aspect of the mailroom, maintain *responsibility* for outcomes and have *permission* to take the right action at the right time.

A team we worked with was under stress. Too many challenges. Not enough resources. Their operational teams were being led by very knowledgeable, committed, and authoritative *managers*. The teams themselves were competent and clearly committed. Yet as teams they were clearly underperforming, error prone, and inefficient and grew even more ineffective after an audit when they were pushed to get better results.

During a leadership coaching assignment with one of the managers, it quickly became apparent that the manager, as well as the others, had assumed absolute authority to direct all the critical activities of their teams because they thought they had to. In doing so, they had underestimated the capability, knowledge, and capacity of individual team members. They didn't know that they didn't know everything. They assumed that authority meant an obligation to give very specific and all-encompassing direction. The consequence was that the teams performed only the tasks included in such binding direction.

I once worked with a chap who boasted that he never had to
fire people, they would quit because of the pain he inflicted on
them. This isn't a principle to be proud of! It wasn't surprising to
me that he didn't last very long in his position. Maybe people like
that are "idiot savants." They get ahead because of some unique
talent or reason, but don't have the right attitudes to lead.

J-P Soublière

Good leaders can maintain the right kinds of dialogues that
allow lots of room for self-expression, while at the same
time not surrendering their status as leaders. This means that
you really have to be sure that you know yourself well.

Rosemarie Leclair

Despite our track record of success, I can honestly say that
we didn't have the best people. We had good people, good
processes, and lots of hard work. It would be lying to say
otherwise. At the same time, I think the company was at least
ten years ahead of the competition (processes, culture, and
market penetration) — that's what good people can do!

J-P Soublière

People are found out pretty quickly. An unsuccessful
leader will not have a following.

Franklin Holtforster

The team members learned a behaviour that was centralized around doing what they were told, not what they knew was required. They had given up thinking for themselves. Their knowledge had no value and they stopped sharing it.

We brought everyone together. We asked them to take the self-assessments (presented next in this chapter) and together we identified a huge unused capacity and store of knowledge that the management team was completely ignoring. They began to understand what they were really good at and gave each other permission to do these things along with the responsibility for doing them well.

The changes in team performance were immediate, dramatic, and emotional. They stopped being a "dumb" team and began to be a "high-performance" team. They acquired specific self-awareness individually and collectively and were able to use their strengths while minimizing the effects of their weaknesses. They continued to be individuals within a strong team. Their self-awareness heightened their understanding of their personality and style, communication techniques, values, vision, technical skills and weaknesses, training needs, family commitments, community involvement . . . The value that emerged was exponentially greater than science could have predicted – a complete turnaround, a team without friction, individuals inspired, performance enhanced.

Some people naturally seek assistance. Often people seek to understand when they experience failure. Either way, people cannot afford to ignore their weaknesses or strengths.

Even the most successful in our society have had some kind of failure. Unless you have failure you cannot learn and develop. It is necessary to experience these events in order to recognize how to correctly deploy your strengths when a situation arises or whom to ask for help to cover your areas of weakness.

We believe that when you put your authority ahead of your authenticity, you will not be inclined to ask for help. On the other hand, when you clearly understand your authentic self, it will be easy and sensible to seek advice from those who have strengths that you do not have. When you think this way, you are beginning to think like a twenty-first-century leader.

Self-Assessment #1 — Self-Knowledge and Authenticity

For each item below, **circle** a rating on the scoring grid that most accurately matches your agreement/disagreement with the statement. Your responses to the questionnaire are for your personal use as you assess and develop your leadership strengths.

	Behaviour, Knowledge, Actions	STRONGLY DISAGREE	DISAGREE	NEUTRAL	AGREE	STRONGLY AGREE
1	I use self-assessment tools to systematically identify my Leadership strengths and weaknesses (the authentic me).	1	2	3	4	5
2	I ensure that an assessment tool is appropriate for the information I seek (self-knowledge).	1	2	3	4	5
3	I ensure that the assessment results are appropriately analyzed.	1	2	3	4	5
4	I engage others to help me interpret results.	1	2	3	4	5
5	I consolidate my Leadership assessment results.	1	2	3	4	5
6	I encourage my peers and subordinates to participate in assessing my skills.	1	2	3	4	5
7	I identify my Leadership needs from information I collect.	1	2	3	4	5
8	I seek other perspectives on my Leadership skills (i.e. non-workplace environments).	1	2	3	4	5
9	I use a workplace-wide perspective to help me understand my Leadership needs and strengths.	1	2	3	4	5
10	When I understand my strengths and needs, I look at them from different angles before taking action.	1	2	3	4	5
	Add the circled scores and enter the sum in the box below					

My Behaviour, Knowledge, Action score means I have:

50–41 Advanced capability	20–11 Opportunities for growth
40–21 Working capability	10–01 Critical need to improve

My key findings:

What do I think my strengths are when it comes to assessing my leadership skills?

1 _____

_____

2 _____

_____

3 _____

_____

What could I do to improve my leadership self-knowledge?

1 _____

_____

2 _____

_____

3 _____

_____

Mentoring at the high end of performance can be quite pleasant but it's really hard work when you're working on the bottom end; but that has to be done too. If you don't follow through at every level, you are going to have a dissatisfied workforce; it's that simple.

Jean Boyle

— — — — — — — — — — — — — — — — — —

A good leader will not introduce expectations that are clearly out of line with reality. If you do that, your team will peg you right away as someone who can't be trusted, can't be believed. They are your followers, not your *stupid* followers.

Jim Durrell

— — — — — — — — — — — — — — — — — —

Once you have a track record of good performance and positive behaviour, the followers find it easier to accept your next challenge. Although I hate to say that you have to "prove yourself," I will.

Shannon Tessier

— — — — — — — — — — — — — — — — — —

Despite the politics and public perception, those who can move the agenda forward are the real leaders.

Rosemarie Leclair

— — — — — — — — — — — — — — — — — —

You will make mistakes. Even Ted Williams batted only .400 or so, and he was the best hitter of all time! That means he missed far more often than he hit the ball! In business, you need to hit much better — like .800 or so. But if you try to bat 1.000, you aren't taking enough chances.

Roger Greenberg

2. Leadership Value Proposition

What is a value proposition? A value proposition is a unique business offering to its customers. It will be why the customer does business with them (or you).

If you were a company selling products, you would be wise to launch a marketing campaign demonstrating the unique value of your products to your customers. This is Marketing 101.

It is generally accepted by marketing experts that most companies — even those that lead the way — struggle to identify the full extent of their value. Even if they identify it, there is a struggle to express it. And, even if it is expressed well, there is no certainty that the customer will "get it."

From a leadership perspective, we face the same challenge. What is our unique leadership value proposition? How do we express it? Is it heard and understood? Does it achieve its intention — that is, to influence people and events to create an outcome greater than science would have predicted?

Our experience with leadership value proposition development has shown us that it is difficult to understand — this is the first challenge.

People may not realize that they should be developing an understanding of their real value. Or they may not take the time. If they do make the effort, our observation is that most of them grossly underestimate their overall leadership value. This could be simple modesty, and sometimes it is. Usually though, it is simply an inability to examine our value in an objective and thorough manner. We simply don't know how to go about it.

For clients who receive leadership coaching, the level of effort to get to even the most basic understanding of the proposition is high. It takes several meetings with a leadership coach, and usually the completion of a series of assessment tools. There are many off-the-shelf tools that will help. As noted earlier, refer to Appendix D for a sample of these self-assessment tools. If you have the opportunity, we recommend that you use them. Included below is a simple tool that we use to facilitate the conversation.

Picking leaders and recruiting talent is difficult. These people are smart. They've got that combination of the skill set to do the function, a personality that works well with people, and they are driven for business results at the same time. It's a blending.

John Watts

Leadership trumps process. Process is important but not too much of it. Every process is up for grabs. When a process doesn't make sense anymore, someone has to stand up and say something's changed or we didn't think this through. It just doesn't make sense anymore.

Jan Kaminski

Leadership may be at times lonely, but you aren't really alone. You aren't leading if you are trying to do it on your own. There have to be followers. Throughout my career in private business and in politics, I've always had great people surrounding me — people whose skills I understood and used.

Jim Durrell

Sometimes leaders fail to see themselves the way others see them. This is a good litmus test. Gauge yourself by the way others see you.

Jim Orban

Sometimes there are those whom the leader simply cannot influence. There are those who are not willing to be led. Perhaps they are not interested in the goal — perhaps we don't share common value.

Shannon Tessier

MAXIMUM VALUE PROPOSITION

Maximum Value Proposition integrates:

- ▶ Personal history and attributes
- ▶ Competitiveness, standards, and confidence
- ▶ Willingness to keep learning while honestly reflecting on past failures and successes
- ▶ Continuous growth _and_ understanding leadership skill, knowledge, and function
- ▶ Strategic and tactical agility in turbulent socio-economic times

Your leadership value proposition will be a combination of the factors shown in the diagram above. At any given time, these factors combine to create your influencing presence, as seen by others. If you are presenting a value proposition that underestimates your real value, your ability to influence is reduced. Similarly, if you overestimate your real value, others will see that, and again your influencing capacity will be reduced; you are simply not a believable leader.

In our experience, the latter is more troublesome and harder to overcome because of the impression it leaves on subordinates or others. We all have met the know-it-all, aggressive individual who attempts to influence but rarely does.

To help clarify the positive aspects of a value proposition, here is an example: Mike Fisher, professional hockey player, Ottawa Senators. Mr. Fisher projects to us a value proposition of wholesomeness, hard work, modesty, and loyalty. The general public assumes, based upon a comparison of this projection and Mr. Fisher's actual behaviour, that this summary is probably accurate. Those who believe that wholesomeness, hard work, modesty, and loyalty are cornerstone values to success will allow Mr. Fisher to influence them. Apparently the community agrees that he is what he appears to be.

In this example, we have someone who likely understands his value and has adopted a pattern of behaviour and presence that is not in conflict with that value, and consequently, his permission to influence us — even if we don't know him

You never should be satisfied with who you are as a leader. Pursue leadership learning but do not ignore the larger business issues. The broader your perspective and the more you work at what it is to be a good leader, ultimately the better you'll be — and the higher an asset you will be for your work, your environment, and your stakeholders.

Jim Orban

I cannot believe that leaders worth anything don't recognize when people are bad or not living up to the values of the job. Why don't they take the steps to fix things? Even in large companies or institutions, it is only a small minority, let's say the top 20 percent, who make the real impact. I guess the question is, are you one of these, and if not, do you want to be one?

J-P Soublière

Letting people realize their full capability is a very important component of a leader's job. This is especially important in a resourced constrained environment when the pool count of talent is limited and recruitment is so competitive.

Franklin Holtforster

Leaders need continuous learning opportunities. At Boeing we had an "on-line" university, mandatory learning goals, regular leadership gatherings, and lots of listening. Boeing was serious about leadership-based success.

Jean Boyle

personally — is in place. This would be a classic example of a public figure whose maximum value proposition works for us.

Just as individuals project, each organization has its own presentation of the value it offers and an intuitive or intentional structure that defines and endorses a value proposition. When our individual leadership value proposition aligns with other individuals or an organization, we find a "good fit." It is this good fit that frees us to influence and be influenced in the best manner possible.

At work, you meet all kinds of people, and if you are in tune with your maximum value proposition, you will be transmitting your fit criteria and you will be able to easily interpret others. Not only will you be able to identify with a group, team, peer, or superior that you are capable of influencing and being influenced by, you will have a finely tuned safety mechanism to identify those whose value proposition is in some way fundamentally in conflict with yours. This could be your "early warning system," identifying those whom you should know better or avoid entirely.

HIGH-PERFORMANCE LEADERSHIP RELATIONSHIPS

My Leader

My Peers   ME   My Peers

My Team

Each high-performance relationship is based upon your leadership value proposition.

The MBA programs and various leadership programs
are built to create leaders in their likeness.

An MBA is after all called a management degree — not a
leadership creativity degree. The notion that simply show me
good financials and I'll show you a leader does not cut it.

Franklin Holtforster

— — — — — — — — — — — — — — — — — —

People are all different. There is no one road map for development.
It is dependent on the individual's competencies, skills, and desire for
development. Often the hardest part is bringing a person to the point
where he wants to develop. Some people just don't want to move
forward. They are comfortable in the present. Change scares them.

Deborah Dickson

— — — — — — — — — — — — — — — — — —

In the important areas of value-based behaviour, there is no
such thing as nine to five. Like it or not, we carry our qualities
with us as we move through life, including our work life.

Shannon Tessier

— — — — — — — — — — — — — — — — — —

Get involved. Walk around. Knowing your people and what they are
doing is fundamental to influencing them to make positive changes. The
good performers will come to you for advice and understanding. Listen
to them carefully but make sure that you never let them off the hook.

Jean Boyle

— — — — — — — — — — — — — — — — — —

You need to identify your best people and lead them well,
because if you don't, someone else certainly will.

Rosemarie Leclair

Another simple truth is that if your behaviour or the way others see you in any way conflicts with who you are (skill conflicts, work value conflicts, character conflicts, behaviour conflicts, mannerism conflicts, and so forth), you are immediately reducing your leadership influence.

A final word about your early warning system; if you listen to it, this system will identify those around you who will represent the best possible working potential; or those around you who have the potential to derail or disrupt your ability to succeed.

Self-Assessment #2 – Leadership Value Proposition

For each item below, **circle** a rating on the scoring grid that most accurately matches your agreement/disagreement with the statement. Your responses to the questionnaire are for your personal use as you assess and develop your leadership strengths.

	Behaviour, Knowledge, Actions	STRONGLY DISAGREE	DISAGREE	NEUTRAL	AGREE	STRONGLY AGREE
1	I understand my specific leadership style and strengths. This is my leadership Value Proposition.	1	2	3	4	5
2	I understand my specific leadership weaknesses.	1	2	3	4	5
3	I understand how and when to apply my Value Proposition.	1	2	3	4	5
4	I understand my personality "blind spots" as they apply to my leadership style.	1	2	3	4	5
5	I understand what it takes to motivate me to willingly deploy my Value Proposition.	1	2	3	4	5
6	I know what keeps me from being my most effective best.	1	2	3	4	5
7	I know what my most effective leadership attribute is.	1	2	3	4	5
8	I know how to use my most powerful leadership styles or attributes.	1	2	3	4	5
9	I understand how and when I learn about improving or enlarging on my Value Proposition.	1	2	3	4	5
10	I know what personal characteristics I have that "maximize" my Value Proposition.	1	2	3	4	5
	Add the circled scores and enter the sum in the box below					

My Behaviour, Knowledge, Action score means I have:

50–41 Advanced capability	20–11 Opportunities for growth
40–21 Working capability	10–01 Critical need to improve

My key findings:

What are my leadership **Value Proposition** components?

1 _____

_____

2 _____

_____

3 _____

_____

What could I do to better understand how to more effectively use my **Value Proposition** strengths?

1 _____

_____

2 _____

_____

3 _____

_____

At the employee level, I talk to every single employee every day, even if it's just to say hello. I want them all to feel part of what we are doing.

Jim Durrell

—————————————————

Simple leadership approaches transcend generations. For a leader to be successful, he has to be in the right time and place for his skills to be effective.

Jim Orban

—————————————————

I want my staff to ask "why?" It makes them better employees if they understand the "why," not just the "what" or the "how." I love it when they ask.

Gerry Arial

—————————————————

All my lunches were planned. I would go from a day with clients to a day with employees (usually four), randomly chosen. I did this to enable two-way communication, exchanging ideas, and exploring attitudes, too. I forced the doors to stay open, not just *say* that they were open, as I had seen others do.

J-P Soublière

—————————————————

Understand the limit of what you can influence. Sort of like the alcoholic's prayer, I guess.

Jim Durrell

3. Vision and Values

If you are a linear learner, you will have completed Themes 1 and 2 and will have reached some conclusions about your self-knowledge and authenticity and your own leadership value proposition. Now it's time to apply this knowledge to your applied leadership approach.

If you have started reading the book at this point, welcome! You are getting down to the heart of things.

It is not necessary to be a leadership expert in all six themes, but it is necessary to understand the relationship that you need to have with your (and your team's, your family's, your community's . . .) values and vision.

Values include what you believe in, what you stand for, and how you behave. Vision includes a clearly understood direction of your effort based upon a combination of your current circumstances, current resources, and insight into future challenges or intentions.

The combination of understood, agreed, and practised values when combined with an understood and agreed vision creates the so-called "page" upon which everyone works from (or at least tries to).

Vision

It is difficult to understand how anyone can go through life without having a destination or a map to get there. There are some people who seem to simply "wander through life" and acquire some success. We think that they are the exception. Could they be more successful? We think so.

Most of us need to understand where we are going, why we are going, and how we are going to get there.

This section combines vision with value. Together, these are the two fundamental ingredients in the leadership cultural framework that governs individual and team behavioural subsequent performance.

Values without an accompanying vision is potential with nowhere to go. It is a family trip without a destination.

I think if I blew a whistle, a very large portion of people who worked for me would come to help me or work for me again.

It would mean that I felt respected, that I did not abuse the relationship, and that I did not abuse the good will we shared.

Franklin Holtforster

You'd better understand both sides of the knowledge grid. It won't be enough to know what you know. You have to build teams of other leaders and managers who know what you don't know. I was a generalist in my business; I surrounded myself with real expertise in operations and other specialties. When we blend this together and stay honest with each other, we can't lose.

Jean Boyle

Connecting value is the common thread that binds the leaders to the followers. These connections are not accidental but flow from the need to associate with those who generally behave as we do.

Shannon Tessier

Keep your vision of things simple. When I was in charge of Public Works at the City, I often said to staff, "If you can look out the window at the city and complain about anything you see, it's probably our problem to fix, so let's fix it."

Rosemarie Leclair

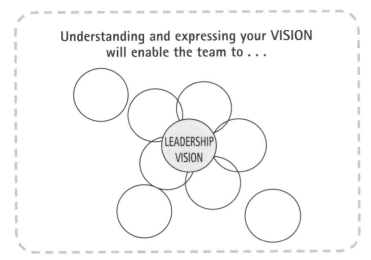

Our definition of applied leadership submits shared vision as a prerequisite for leading and following. We see vision as something as simple as the intention to have a good day, or as complex as a national strategy for environmental management, or anything in between or anything beyond.

It is often required for business or team visions to be facilitated, or brainstormed, or "think-tanked," or "conference-boarded." What is important is that some future state is defined and agreed upon.

Obviously, each leader defines future conditions that are appropriate for themselves and their followers. Appropriateness might be simply getting the team through the next week. It could be to create the best service centre ever. It could be to ensure that a combat unit gets through its next tour. It could be to complete a project or to double the revenues of a corporation. Or, it could be a vision for a thousand-mile wall in China.

One of the characteristics of a powerful vision is that the vision is in response to some compelling need; a need in turn endorsed by the values of the group.

A second characteristic is that the vision is properly interpreted so that every person in the group understands it in his own way at his own level. No matter if you are high in the hierarchy or at the bottom, you have had an opportunity to hear and reflect the vision. Your version is in line with everyone else's.

Basically, we've done a dreadful job of providing succession plans for the senior leaders of the company. We're trying to change that over the next two years. We need to preserve and develop our people, our high achievers, those with high potential. They're already here and are committed to our vision. We have to help them grow.

Roger Greenberg

When I have been wrong in my leadership or in my vision, it has consistently been when I abandoned my sense of realism for an unsubstantiated level of optimism. There are times when walls are too thick to break and too high to climb. You need to recognize this and find solutions that will work within the context in which you find yourself. To do otherwise would lead to the destruction of you and your followers.

Jim Durrell

If you lose sight of the personal and corporate values that your employees thought were fundamental, don't be shocked when your corporation falls apart.

You simply cannot abandon the values and ethics that you establish in an organization. To do so is to abandon your leadership responsibility. Don't expect your followers to follow after that.

Jean Boyle

When you lay out your vision of the "Promised Land," lay out the right message. In my business the promised land is where we stick together, take care of our families, get a decent paycheque, stick up for each other. It's all we can do. Although the leader has to push the limits, it is absolutely required that he or she stay within the boundaries of what he/she believes to be real. Trust is based upon this consistency.

Jim Durrell

A third characteristic is that the leader provides a vision that generally can be supported by the skills and processes that are available. We hesitate with this last point because we know that some of the great things that have happened and will happen are in response to visions that call upon resources and skills that do not yet exist.

The day-to-day reality is that our personal and team vision is governed by the realities of the day. We are big believers in expressing "working outside the box" but we are realistic enough to realize that for most of us, just getting the work done inside the box is challenge enough, especially when somebody is continually resizing the box.

Values

Talking about our values is not easy. Most people embrace their value set but, when asked to articulate them, find it difficult to focus on specifics with context and priority. Values are important to our definition of applied leadership:

> **APPLIED LEADERSHIP IS . . .**
>
> . . . intentional
> . . . direct
> . . . *influences*
>
> those who share *our*
>
> **VISION _and_ VALUES**
>
> **APPLIED LEADERSHIP CREATES . . .**
> a result greater than that possible
> by using management science alone

Simply put, applied leadership assumes that there is a sharing of core values amongst the organization members, the leadership, and the followers. The intention of the leader is to promote followers to independently take the right actions to achieve the results required. A leader must have the confidence to believe that the actions will remain consistent with the core values. Even when mistakes do occur, forgiveness and correction is easy – when the values have not been violated.

A leader must be able to intuit the changes coming. Maybe no one else sees it, but you need to. Trust your intuition and understand how to read trends. You will be handling a lot of unique challenges. It will be a learning process for everyone. In the end it must make sense.

Jim Orban

It is the role of the leader to look forward, to determine what's coming, and to decide what to do about it. The leader maintains competitiveness while being responsible for all the people who depend on them.

Franklin Holtforster

Even when you are sticking to your guns, your values, and so on, you might not sleep well at night. It's a heavy burden to draw the line when others will not.

J-P Soublière

You build respect by bringing a genuine respect for others.

France Jacovella

Generational differences are real. We are what we have experienced in our lifetimes. But you know, even with these differences, people still respond to the leadership influence regardless of the generation it comes from. People are people. There is one differentiator that applies to the current generation, however, and that is that they "text" better than they write.

Jim Durrell

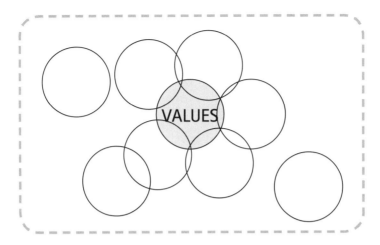

Understanding your values, your team's values, your organization's values, etc. and where they match, overlap, or miss entirely will give you a foundation for influencing or a clear indication of where you will have to put some leadership effort in order find a common basis for value agreement.

Here are the kinds of values we are talking about. First the obvious: integrity, honesty, generosity, passion, trust, trustworthiness, devotion, and loyalty. Now, some that are not so obvious: enterprise, candidness, dignity, discretion, prudence, realism, shrewdness, and tact.

The challenge for individuals and teams is to have an open conversation that determines, from the examples above and many more, which key values represent the team and everyone in it. The importance of choosing exactly those values that represent the group and that the group can live up to cannot be overemphasized.

Take your time. Have a list. Encourage the debate. Make sure that everyone understands exactly what each value selected really means.

This is not a simple discussion and should not be skipped! Remember, "**Wehn Tinhgs Go Wrnog!**" seventy-five percent of the time, failure will occur when the care and feeding of the value set for the leader and the team has been abandoned.

Here's an example of how important and complex this issue can be. We worked with a client, a senior member of a very successful manufacturer, whose character was then and is now

I want a relationship of trust and respect, but we don't have
to be best friends. A leader needs to hear and accept what you
actually think, not what you think the leader wants to hear.

Rosemarie Leclair

— — — — — — — — — — — — — — — — —

There is no such thing as a stupid idea. I want to hear
what you've got to say. You might get told no, because . . .
And you might not like what I have to say. But at least
everybody has a voice. Everybody doesn't get a vote.

John Watts

— — — — — — — — — — — — — — — — —

Tons of brilliant people with wonderful visions have completely
stumbled because they either had no one to tell the vision to who
would believe it, or they didn't have the basic communication skills
already in place to get the message across in the first place.

Jim Durrell

— — — — — — — — — — — — — — — —

A leader must be respectful. Respect is a word you hear all
the time, but what does it mean? It is not just a word. There
are some basic attributes that can be built upon that will
make you a better leader, and respect is one of them.

Jim Orban

— — — — — — — — — — — — — — — —

I've always had this notion that between workers and management,
union or non-union, there has to be a respectful relationship expressed
between them. And I've tried to promote that. We need to understand
that there can be legitimate disagreements, but disagreement
expressed in disrespectful ways leaves wounds that are tough to heal.

Rosemarie Leclair

above reproach and whose attention to detail and expertise in the corporation's market share was second to none. One of the values that this executive constantly projected onto the team was meticulousness. It was clear that this leader imposed meticulousness ahead of every other value, including timeliness and collaboration. The team ended up with perfect deliverables that were never available on time for consideration by the other executives.

Was their intention good? Absolutely. Did this executive construct a team with the appropriate value fundamentals? Absolutely not. Did the team get the chance to help the executive modify team behaviour to meet the requirements? No. They did not have a collaborative forum to discuss value fundamentals. Was it easy to fix? Yes.

The bottom line on values is that they are very easy to talk about and very hard to consistently live up to. Not having the conversation at all is the biggest mistake a leader can make.

In the section on Building Trust, we connect the dots on how consistently operating against a value set is a fundamental of the trust needed between followers and leaders.

Self-Assessment #3 — Vision and Values

For each item below, **circle** a rating on the scoring grid that most accurately matches your agreement/disagreement with the statement. Your responses to the questionnaire are for your personal use as you assess and develop your leadership strengths.

	Behaviour, Knowledge, Actions	STRONGLY DISAGREE	DISAGREE	NEUTRAL	AGREE	STRONGLY AGREE
1	I can describe a personal vision (for my future) that is achievable with the assets available to me now.	1	2	3	4	5
2	I can detail the personal values that I practise that I would never trade away.	1	2	3	4	5
3	I know that those I lead share most if not all of the values I live by.	1	2	3	4	5
4	I know that my superiors understand and endorse my personal vision.	1	2	3	4	5
5	I work to ensure that my team has a shared vision of our future together and that the vision is achievable with the assets available to us now.	1	2	3	4	5
6	When anyone I work with behaves outside our established value set, I do not ignore or endorse that behaviour.	1	2	3	4	5
7	I create regular opportunities for all of us to have "brainstorm" discussions about our vision and to help develop action plans and priorities to achieve it.	1	2	3	4	5
8	I create opportunities to "brainstorm" our values in order to promote clarity about what we stand for.	1	2	3	4	5
9	I follow the action plans developed to support our vision of the future.	1	2	3	4	5
10	I communicate our values in my words and deeds.	1	2	3	4	5
	Add the circled scores and enter the sum in the box below					

My Behaviour, Knowledge, Action score means I have:

50–41 Advanced capability	20–11 Opportunities for growth
40–21 Working capability	10–01 Critical need to improve

My key findings:

What is my **vision** and how am I working to make it a reality?

1 _____

_____

2 _____

_____

3 _____

_____

Do I stick to my **values** (even when it's not popular or convenient)? What difference does that make to me and others?

1 _____

_____

2 _____

_____

3 _____

_____

Sometimes I try too hard to fix employee problems. I've discovered that if the problems are character, lifestyle, or value based, I may not be able to help and I have to limit my effort. These employees have always created the most disruption and the least satisfaction for me.

Rob Lindsay

You have to trust your sense of what the "right thing to do" is, and if it turns out to be not so right, change it!

J-P Soublière

Leadership is messy. It isn't always clear-cut. You want people to be straying outside the lines.

Franklin Holtforster

We made values very simple and always visible, so that we were surrounded every day as we walked around.

Jacquelin Holzman

Achieving your numbers and your objectives is certainly important, but the way you get there is equally important. Quality counts!

Rosemarie Leclair

Develop a good, basic planning framework for your Team — vision, goals, etc. — and then work on it continuously to keep pace with what's happening.

Rob Lindsay

4. Coaching Others and Collaboration

This theme is all about Rule #1.

> **LEADERSHIP RULE #1**
> I promise to make you better, *and*
> you promise to do your part.

If you are going to be a successful leader in this turbulent century, get used to the idea that you will be coaching continuously during the everyday interactions between you and your team, your peers, and perhaps even your superiors. This is where you turn your experience, knowledge, education, and skills into instruments that can identify where you need to be introducing new ideas, translating future challenges, guiding skilled resources, facilitating discussions, motivating, consolidating gain, celebrating victories, resolving conflicts, and so forth. You will be coaching and collaborating.

If you have not yet developed a coaching and collaboration approach, now is the time. Employees in the twenty-first century have more information and power than ever before. Your role as leader is to help guide them to use these tools in the most appropriate and powerful way. From what we see, this may be the principal method that can keep teams performing at a high pace while maintaining the required agility and information sharing that is required in these times.

If you are going to coach others to a higher level, your first responsibility is to understand your own knowledge and skill limitations along with your strengths. This goes back to the "know what you know and don't know" concept.

Your second responsibility is to provide the time, information, and tools to allow employees to have as full control as possible over their careers and to be encouraged to understand their MVP and how it might be applied to help the team reach its goals.

These are your responsibilities, but the recipients of these opportunities and this knowledge have a clear responsibility as

When you lead, you will make mistakes. Own up to them and move on. Learn from those errors. Get the best people to get the best information and you'll get better decisions. Even with Gen X/Y, give them the best info, the best values, and they'll make good decisions.

Jacquelin Holzman

Sometimes helping someone to find something else, somewhere else, with somebody else, is the best leadership move possible.

Shannon Tessier

This is about listening and accountability. You've got a commitment from them about what you want to do. They in turn help you and the organization and understand their role.

John Watts

Let's put things in the right order. Teach your employees, give them tools and room to create, don't make things driven by the factory approach. Sometimes you won't see the immediate profit in that approach but in the long term you will have built something worthwhile.

Gerry Arial

I think that leaders invest in people and quality in order to get the best possible profit and loss outcome.

Rob Lindsay

well. The degree to which they embrace your offer determines the degree to which they intend to earn the growth and opportunity you are offering. In this applied leadership world, no one gets "off the hook."

Coaching is a skill and can be developed through example and structured learning. Most often associated with sport, but now recognized as an essential tool in the twenty-first-century workplace, coaching skill development needs to be a high personal and corporate priority.

Increasingly, organizations are bringing in professional coaches. This can be a way of accelerating coaching skill development as well as providing a safe and confidential source for executive development. We have seen the value of both internal mentoring and external coaching.

In the end, you and your organization must find a way to train and maintain internal coaching resources. This could be a component of the leadership cultural framework that is added specifically to accelerate the coaching process.

Collaboration amongst high-value individuals and groups is another key capability-building and problem-solving tool. It is emerging as one of the most important of the many communication capabilities. Social networking is in fact a massive and worldwide collaboration effort that generates extraordinary transfers of information, good and bad, real and – unfortunately – unreal.

And whether we like it or not, formal or informal collaboration can generate great opportunities and severe challenges.

Numerous people and organizations have studied collaboration techniques and their effects. There are many good sources of information and research that are all accessible on the Internet or at a local bookstore. These sources can provide insight and valuable process tools and guidance to permit you to take full advantage of a collaborative approach while minimizing the risks of the high pace of information transfer (especially disinformation).

As part of your value proposition and its requirement for continuous learning, we suggest that you invest some time and investigate the latest independent work on collaborative techniques. You will find the information immediately useful.

Make your leadership decisions all about making things better for others. Any other reason is just not going to cut it!

Jean Boyle

— — — — — — — — — — — — — — — — — —

The good leaders don't let us off the hook but they always offer their understanding. They offer practical ways for us to get back into the groove, to regain our enthusiasm, to get back to accomplishing what we can. This is when the leader's experience really pays off.

Shannon Tessier

— — — — — — — — — — — — — — — — — —

When I commanded a base, I insisted that all my subordinates do the right thing for their staff. I knew it wasn't getting done at first and I knew we had to live up to our responsibilities as leaders. Industry, as it turns out, is no different.

Jean Boyle

— — — — — — — — — — — — — — — —

Development is the most important aspect of leadership but is not training. Training, per my definition, contributes the hard skills for the job. Development provides broadening and stretching opportunities for the individual through assignments, projects, teamwork, exposure, coaching, mentoring, and self-awareness.

Deborah Dickson

— — — — — — — — — — — — — — — —

I looked at everyone I hired as someone who could take my job next week or in five years. A leader cannot be afraid of having smarter people working for him or her.

Dave Dickson

Fundamental to either successful coaching or collaboration is the ability to communicate effectively, which has two dimensions: the clarity of the message from the sender and the willingness and ability to listen by the receiver. Whether you are sending or receiving, the clarity and intention of your messages are constantly being filtered and adjusted. In the diagram we show some of the possible filters that might be in play.

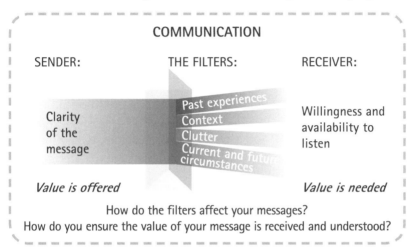

COMMUNICATION

SENDER: THE FILTERS: RECEIVER:

Clarity   Past experiences   Willingness and
of the   Context   availability to
message   Clutter   listen
                           Current and future
                           circumstances

Value is offered   *Value is needed*

How do the filters affect your messages?
How do you ensure the value of your message is received and understood?

Past experiences, context, distractions, and circumstances are all filters, which can and often do deflect, warp, or garble what we say or how we hear what others are saying to us. If there was ever a circumstance that demands the need for leaders to understand their need to translate carefully, this is it.

Often leaders face situations where they have presented ideas or material comprehensively and coherently in their own minds and discover later that no one heard the message. Or, if they heard it, they have applied filters that completely distorted the original intent.

You will have to use formal and informal communication methods to get your message out and to test that it's being received correctly. One technique emphasized by our leadership interviewees was "LBWA" – "Leading by Walking Around." The LBWA advantage is that the leader can bridge the gap between her message and the receiver through informal discussion, by encouraging and listening to feedback (from the horse's mouth) and by setting a visible example of what she had in mind.

Whether it be with a group, on a stage, in a meeting, or even in one-on-one situations, your success will depend on your ability to get your message across. This is an area of skill and confidence that we all need to work on because it is so fundamental.

Shannon Tessier

— — — — — — — — — — — — — — — — — —

Focus on the decision process first and not the messaging required to promote the decision. If you can't find the correct message, perhaps the decision is wrong! Leadership effort succeeds through "buy-in," after all. If you aren't convinced yourself, start over.

Rosemarie Leclair

— — — — — — — — — — — — — — — — —

There is nothing worse than telling someone, "Here are your goals for the year." But he had nothing to do with creating them. He accepts them because the boss told him. You should sit down together and say, "Here are some things I want to achieve in the coming year. What can you do to help me get there?" The person may phrase his goals in such a way that they are way more meaningful to him, and they achieve your end objective.

John Watts

— — — — — — — — — — — — — — — — —

When you are communicating well and effectively, you get to understand immediately when even small things are going adrift. You are able to take action early before you are overwhelmed. Communication allows you to get "out in front."

Jim Durrell

LEADERSHIP RULE #3

I promise to celebrate our successes
in public and discuss our failures in private
and I ask you to do the same.

This would also be an opportunity to exercise Leadership Rule #3. The coach and collaborator will find many opportunities to communicate as required in public or in private.

Self-Assessment #4 — Coaching and Collaboration

For each item below, **circle** a rating on the scoring grid that most accurately matches your agreement/disagreement with the statement. Your responses to the questionnaire are for your personal use as you assess and develop your leadership strengths.

	Behaviour, Knowledge, Actions	STRONGLY DISAGREE	DISAGREE	NEUTRAL	AGREE	STRONGLY AGREE
1	I take seriously my responsibility to **coach/mentor** others in my work team.	1	2	3	4	5
2	I intentionally invest specific periods of time for people's development.	1	2	3	4	5
3	When I'm **coaching**, I make sure that my **coaching** role is clearly defined.	1	2	3	4	5
4	When I'm **coaching**, I'm working on specific changes/improvements/outcomes.	1	2	3	4	5
5	I create real opportunity for others to test/assess their leadership skills.	1	2	3	4	5
6	I help people find/use opportunities to earn more leadership responsibility.	1	2	3	4	5
7	I actively look for ways to identify success opportunities for others.	1	2	3	4	5
8	I help people take advantage of new leadership challenges.	1	2	3	4	5
9	I make sure that those whom I mentor understand my expectations.	1	2	3	4	5
10	I create with others leadership **coaching** plans that include criteria for success.	1	2	3	4	5
	Add the circled scores and enter the sum in the box below					

My Behaviour, Knowledge, Action score means I have:

50–41 Advanced capability	20–11 Opportunities for growth
40–21 Working capability	10–01 Critical need to improve

My key findings:

What will others say my strengths are as a **coach** or mentor?

1 _____

_____

2 _____

_____

3 _____

_____

What are my most challenging situations when developing leadership improvement in others?

1 _____

_____

2 _____

_____

3 _____

_____

When someone does a good job, even it is just helping a colleague, writing a great letter, chairing well a meeting, tell her. It is important to give feedback as it happens — right then and there.

France Jacovella

Celebration is one aspect of humanism in a leader. In an active leadership role, it is the crystallization of faith. Evidence of celebration and constructive criticism should always allow the other person to respond. Open communication is essential. We put a bell in each office that can be rung when we have won something. It works — they ring!

Franklin Holtforster

If you never make mistakes, it means you do things the proven way. If you never take chances, it means you are not thinking outside the box. A leader must offer forgiveness for mistakes, to enable people to learn from them.

France Jacovella

While we celebrate in public, we criticize in private. I honour this rule in every aspect. Leaders not only have to sometimes criticize, they also have to be adult enough to take criticism back.

Criticism means "to critique" — which is a positive exchange. Unfortunately, the word has become negative in our society.

Franklin Holtforster

5. Building Trust

High-performance teams in this century are completely dependent on each team member's understanding and deploying his or her MVP in line with the leadership cultural framework that the team has adopted.

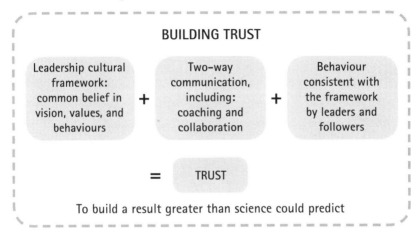

BUILDING TRUST

| Leadership cultural framework: common belief in vision, values, and behaviours | **+** | Two-way communication, including: coaching and collaboration | **+** | Behaviour consistent with the framework by leaders and followers |

=   TRUST

To build a result greater than science could predict

This dependency is driven by the change rate, which often requires independent and unsupervised actions. Without trust this dependency is not possible. The sequential steps shown above are drawn from our applied leadership research and form the foundation of trusting team relationships.

Given the explosion of information available, it is evident that we must be capable of taking action when the information is available to us – even if the information available is less than complete. There needs to be a level of trust not only between team members, but each member must also trust himself. Each member must understand his own and his team's strengths and limitations and be able to accept the consequences of the actions the team takes.

In the new workplace, the leader needs to be able to trust the team to always act in accordance with the agreed cultural framework and

Even the best leaders will make mistakes. The errors that cannot be forgiven are the ones that violate trust, were not properly acknowledged, and were never put right.

Shannon Tessier

Be ready and able to separate the politics from your operations. The leader must present thorough, thoughtful, and well-reasoned advice while maintaining loyalty and trust. Your direction and advice must reflect the long-term view and the staying power to deliver that the politics of the moment cannot!

Rosemarie Leclair

As a leader, one of the most challenging things is to make sure that your message gets out clearly. You have to communicate with all employees, and that is hard.

John Watts

The ability to build relationships is fundamental to leadership. People need to trust and feel like they are part of a positive relationship. They need to feel the integrity, the desire for achievement. They need to feel all of those things that are important to building a relationship. If you get that right, people will follow.

Jim Durrell

Leaders need to see urgency and act on it, even if it means stretching beyond what others anticipate from them.

Jim Orban

must accept and forgive errors when they inevitably occur. Since it is more important to act than to wait for more information, trust and confidence are required to be at the core of a team's operational capacity.

Figuratively speaking, the leader today is continuously handing over the keys to the car with the belief that the destination has been understood and agreed and trusting that the followers will get there safely and on time.

TIPS FOR BUILDING TRUST

Trust takes time to build. Tips for building trust include:

- ▶ Honour diversity of thinking, learning, and other individual differences.
- ▶ Don't make promises you can't keep.
- ▶ Keep your commitment.
- ▶ Maintain confidences.
- ▶ Value each person's inputs and ideas.
- ▶ Be honest.
- ▶ Use good people skills.
- ▶ Use good facilitation skills.
- ▶ Eliminate blame.

Although trust is built slowly, it can be destroyed in an instant, and when it has been destroyed, rebuilding trust takes a very long time.

A final thought: sometimes the best route that followers can take will be driven by their collective MVP, and not necessarily rigidly by a map and route provided by the leader.

Self-Assessment #5 – Building Trust

For each item below, **circle** a rating on the scoring grid that most accurately matches your agreement/disagreement with the statement. Your responses to the questionnaire are for your personal use as you assess and develop your leadership strengths.

	Behaviour, Knowledge, Actions	STRONGLY DISAGREE	DISAGREE	NEUTRAL	AGREE	STRONGLY AGREE
1	I know some good ways to **build trust** with others.	1	2	3	4	5
2	I provide opportunities to make it safe for others to say what's on their minds.	1	2	3	4	5
3	I create a culture/expectation of forgiveness and assistance when others fail despite their best efforts.	1	2	3	4	5
4	I am sure that our work standards have been defined and published.	1	2	3	4	5
5	I accept work results/solutions when they meet the work standards, even though they may represent different solutions to problems than I would have chosen.	1	2	3	4	5
6	When I've established new team goals, I lay out a full framework of expectations and required behaviours.	1	2	3	4	5
7	I create working relationships with others based upon common intentions.	1	2	3	4	5
8	I protect my people against those who want to "hijack" the collaborative effort to their personal goals.	1	2	3	4	5
9	I "walk the talk." I do what I say I will do.	1	2	3	4	5
10	I openly and regularly congratulate and compliment success, effort, and achievement, to the broadest audience possible.	1	2	3	4	5
	Add the circled scores and enter the sum in the box below					

My Behaviour, Knowledge, Action score means I have:

50–41 Advanced capability	20–11 Opportunities for growth
40–21 Working capability	10–01 Critical need to improve

My key findings:

Do I live up to the commitments I've made to others? Examples...

1 _____

_____

2 _____

_____

3 _____

_____

What are the areas of trust development that I need to work on the most? How could I do that?

1 _____

_____

2 _____

_____

3 _____

_____

Listening is key. You need to learn from others why things are going the way they are going. You can't provide a map to make things better if you don't know where you are to start with. In order to enable high performance, it's necessary to understand the motivation, goals, and capacity of those you are influencing, mentoring, leading.

Rob Lindsay

Leaders must have a vision of where it is necessary to go. They have to be able to articulate this vision in bite-sized chunks and inspire others to connect the dots on their own.

Rosemarie Leclair

When you have discussions with staff, you simply cannot multi-task. Keep focused, keep eye contact, and listen. People's work is important! You can't have an eye on the screen of your computer or be texting at the same time as you are talking to someone. Good leaders are respectful!

Roger Greenberg

You can lead some people out of poor performance. It comes back to the individual. You'll find a lot of individuals are in denial.

John Watts

You can't just talk all day. First you build relationships, then you communicate the reality really well, and finally, the leader makes the decisions.

Jim Durrell

6. Credibility and Authority

We need to deploy both credibility and authority in the twenty-first century. We need credibility to establish our right to lead and we need authority to execute this right.

Credibility must be built. Authority is handed down. Both are essential for success.

CREDIBILITY AND AUTHORITY

Built up:	Handed down:
▲ Performance history (experience)	▼ Mandated (role and scope)
▲ Demonstrated skills	▼ Governance
▲ Education	▼ Legislated
▲ Personal value set	▼ Procedures and guidelines
▲ Believer networks	▼ Negotiated (union)
▲ Consistently applied leadership traits	▼ Societal (diversity, gender, cultural)

CREDIBILITY   AUTHORITY

You need both in balance

To put this in context, let's examine the possible extremes. Imagine you are put into an authoritative position where you have no previous experience or credibility. Who will listen to you? Likely no one. Where does your power to influence relationships come from? Not from authority. If it did, all anyone would need is the presence of a demagogue and a rulebook.

Authority without credibility can be temporarily effective in certain extreme circumstances over very short periods of time, but if you are looking for sustained high performance, authority by itself won't last. It is not sustainable.

Credibility without authority is the opposite extreme. The inspirational and credible leader who has no authority to effect change will find it difficult or perhaps impossible to succeed in the end. Influence through credibility exists in all aspects

Leadership is reacting to a series of gaps. If you see the water rising, then you'd better find more sandbags or a boat. Leaders are able to identify gaps and how big they are. Then they figure out what to do and how much time there is to do it.

Jim Orban

When we entrusted the screening of our employees to the most reliable and trusted of the existing employees, we were trying to ensure that we hired only those who could help us maintain the right culture of hard and honest work. We called this the "Bob Gainey" principle. Gainey wasn't the biggest goal scorer, but he became the heart of his hockey team. That's what we wanted. We wanted "salt of the earth, humble employees," and Gainey was the visible model we chose.

J-P Soublière

Stay visible with your workforce. Be recognizable and approachable. Every job, every task, every person needs to feel connected to the leadership, if you are to achieve ultimate success.

Rosemarie Leclair

Good leaders look behind and there is nobody there — they are marching alongside. People who offhandedly describe themselves as good leaders say, "Let's charge off over there." The real test is if they look around them and everyone is there beside them. Another analogy — you blow your whistle for everybody to get out of the pool and they do.

Jim Orban

of society but these people are often heard but not listened to. (Environmental debates are illuminated by the credible, but without authority not much happens.)

Ideally you would like to have both credibility and authority in balance, but it is rare to see someone who has this complete profile. You do not necessarily have to have the full combination, but you have to understand your gaps in either area. For authority shortfalls, speak to your superior and get them filled. Seek redress of the authority gaps through explanations to your superior on how those gaps are preventing you and your team from performing highly. For example, if your group is being criticized for overspending, and you have not been delegated the authority to manage those expenditures, it's not likely that you will be able to resolve the issues quickly, if at all.

On the credibility side, you might be missing some aspect of experience, training, or exposure. You need to identify those gaps and obtain that experience by partnering with a subordinate, a peer, or a superior to obtain that knowledge, or by asking for personal development.

To develop credibility in others is a main goal for twenty-first-century leaders. One of the skills that you will want to develop is that of delegation. Just as you require the appropriate amount of credibility and authority, so do your subordinates. Build their credibility by delegating your authority. You do not delegate the tasks. You delegate the authority to address the tasks.

Self-Assessment #6 — Credibility and Authority

For each item below, **circle** a rating on the scoring grid that most accurately matches your agreement/disagreement with the statement. Your responses to the questionnaire are for your personal use as you assess and develop your leadership strengths.

	Behaviour, Knowledge, Actions	STRONGLY DISAGREE	DISAGREE	NEUTRAL	AGREE	STRONGLY AGREE
1	When I have authoritative power, I use it responsibly.	1	2	3	4	5
2	I take open responsibility for the authority I have now.	1	2	3	4	5
3	I share my power as a means of increasing it.	1	2	3	4	5
4	I offer people an active role in the decision-making processes that affect them.	1	2	3	4	5
5	I acknowledge the credibility of others.	1	2	3	4	5
6	I use the situational credibility of others by giving them power in those areas.	1	2	3	4	5
7	I promote self-confidence in others.	1	2	3	4	5
8	I criticize and correct in private.	1	2	3	4	5
9	I offer opportunities for those who have stumbled in their roles and tasks to redeem themselves.	1	2	3	4	5
10	I accept that my authority and leadership behaviour can also be influenced by others, even those who are subordinate to me.	1	2	3	4	5
	Add the circled scores and enter the sum in the box below					

My Behaviour, Knowledge, Action score means I have:

50–41 Advanced capability	20–11 Opportunities for growth
40–21 Working capability	10–01 Critical need to improve

My key findings:

Do I understand the difference between my influencing power based on **authority** and that which is based upon my personal and professional **credibility**?

1 _____

_____

2 _____

_____

3 _____

_____

Do I overuse one or the other (**credibility or authority**) and if I do, how might I achieve a more balanced influencing style?

1 _____

_____

2 _____

_____

3 _____

_____

SECTION FOUR

Bringing It All Together

So where are we now? We have focused on the individual parts of what we call applied leadership. By now you have been introduced to some of the challenges that are unique to this century and their impact on individuals and organizations. You have also looked at the basic requirements for leadership on the ground.

From the research we have done, we know that the six advanced applied leadership themes are also critical to coping and performing in these circumstances.

Let us now move step by step to bring all the parts together to enable you and eventually your teams to move toward the highest and best performance possible. These steps will help to identify and activate your and your team's Maximum Value Proposition. Your goal is to produce a greater result than science would have predicted again and again and again.

LEADERSHIP CULTURAL FRAMEWORK BUILDING PLAN

1. Conceptualize
2. Design
3. Build
4. Activate
5. Measure and Improve

What follows is a series of steps to bring your applied leadership vision to life and to enable you to do it again and again.

Step 1. Conceptualize your applied leadership vision

Step 2. Design your framework

Step 3. Build your framework

Step 4. Activate and deploy your framework

Step 5. Monitor and improve your framework and vision

Step 1. Conceptualize your applied leadership vision

There are six distinct steps to establish your applied leadership vision:

▶ **Self-knowledge**–Have I completed my "KWYK/KWYDK" grid? Have I completed all six self-assessments? Have I identified my leadership strengths and the opportunities for my development? Have I completed the Section 3 Assessments?

▶ **Environment**–Have I identified my short-, medium-, and long-term challenges and objectives? Can I translate these challenges and objectives to others–superiors, peers, and subordinates? Have I completed the Leadership Vision and Environmental Plan in Appendix A?

▶ **Urgency**–Do I understand the urgency of the challenges I face? Am I able to transmit that urgency to others in an honest and clear way?

▶ **Believers**–Have I identified those who believe in me? Do they understand what I see and their role in helping me to accomplish it?

▶ **Leadership vision**–Can I see clearly the outcome? Have I written it down? Do I know what success looks like?

▶ **Communication**–Do I understand my communication strengths and the potential mechanisms to deliver my messages?

Step 2. Design your framework

Moving from concept to design allows you to begin the process of testing and validating your ideas, goals, and priorities in a sensible and practical way. You are designing the page upon which your leadership script will be written. This is the point to bring in your collaborators (supervisor, peers, subordinates, coalition) to help bring some perspective and to ensure that your leadership goals are based on reality. Adjust your concept(s) as you go. Here's the checklist:

▶ **Anchor your strategic plan.** Secure an agreement on the future from your superior(s). Make sure you are on the same page with them with respect to goals, priorities, resources, and timing and urgency.

▶ **Walk through your leadership vision**

   With peers: Take the leadership vision for the future developed in concept and modified with your superior(s) and present it to your entire peer group. Tap into the expertise and talent of those around you to refine it. Make sure the things you now are planning are appropriate to the peer group (e.g., no unnecessary overlaps). You are actually getting their support as well as getting their advice. Do they clearly understand and endorse your view of your team's future state, including strategic challenges and resource factors (time, money, talent)?

   With subordinates: Using the leadership vision as a base, consult your subordinates and allow them to brainstorm with you to ensure that the future goals, priorities, and general effort take advantage of team strengths while minimizing the risks of team weaknesses. Do they convey to you their assessment of the consequences of the vision? Are you listening?

   With stakeholders: Identify those key stakeholders who will be affected by your goals, priorities, timing, and urgency. Work with them to identify potential roadblocks, success factors, and dis-satisfiers. Can you accommodate the needs of stakeholders in your final plan?

With non-believers: Share and explain your modified leadership vision with those most likely to critique or be critical. Do not defend! Listen with an open mind. Ask questions. Revisit consequences and risks. This is your last chance to modify your design before building it into a leadership framework.

▶ **Consolidate your vision** – Redraft, as required, the concept, taking into account the adjustments from the advice that you have received and accepted.

Step 3. Build your framework

You are not alone anymore. All the building, activation, and measuring steps that follow involve you and your team, as a minimum.

Your leadership cultural framework includes:

▶ Consolidated leadership vision – the one you have spent time conceptualizing and designing

▶ Environment – a description of where the organization wants to be with respect to leadership

▶ Values and Behaviours – an agreed-upon set of working values and supporting behaviours by which everyone operates and is held accountable. This includes agreed limits of permission and forgiveness.

▶ Current team capabilities and capacity SWOT – leadership *and* management capabilities

▶ Leadership impacts on the succession plan

▶ Leadership development plan(s) – individual and team

▶ Leadership impacts on the recruitment and retention strategy

▶ Leadership *and* management performance measurement tools and processes

The integration of these elements into a homogeneous framework is your objective. You can do this with your team by: *Translating the future state and what success will look like based upon your consolidated leadership vision.*

▶ Confirming the organizational and work context – have you forgotten anything?

▶ Establishing team and individual strengths and areas for development as a team and for individuals

▶ Discussing and establishing behavioural norms

▶ Setting the limits for permission and forgiveness

▶ Establishing a consistent team value set

▶ Developing mechanisms for Leadership Rules #1, #2, and #3

▶ Establishing an agreed-upon monitoring and measurement process

▶ Building mechanisms for leadership and management performance assessment, etc.

▶ Creating a clear, written, and accessible record of the critical outcomes – vision, values, behaviours

▶ Establishing for each team member a sensible leadership development plan that will meet both the organization's and the individual's needs (e.g., coaching, training, assignment, formal education, mentoring, etc.)

Step 4. Activate and deploy your framework

Activation means you and everyone on your team are on the same leadership cultural page at the same time and able to answer the following questions:

▶ What is included and does it work?

▶ How is it integrated into the management processes and leadership style?

▶ Does it exist at all levels? If not, why not?

▶ How do you talk about it and use it?

▶ Is it safe to talk about it?

▶ Who is the keeper?

▶ Who is the inspirational source?

▶ How is it kept alive? Is there a feedback loop?

▶ How is it measured?

▶ How will you know if you are successful?

The next step is deployment. The Leadership Cultural Framework becomes your foundation. It is the key reference point – for recruitment, selection, retention, performance, promotion, and succession.

Step 5. Monitor and improve your framework and vision

Monitoring and improvement can be as simple as regularly scheduled leadership conversations where the topic is the framework, how it is being utilized, and whether it is still relevant or in need of rethinking. This leadership conversation could be internal or assisted by external advisors – it doesn't matter how you get this done, but the conversation, in itself, is essential.

To determine the effectiveness of your framework across each of the areas (recruitment, selection, retention, performance, promotion, and succession) will be a challenge. Employee surveys, customer satisfaction surveys, grievances, and employee engagement reviews are all legitimate pointers. Make no mistake – this is about people, feelings, inspiration, motivation, and connectivity. The only way that is close to getting you the true picture will be to continually conduct intentional conversations at all levels concerning the framework, its legitimacy, and the commitment to it by everyone.

This is an ongoing process that requires discipline and focus but has an enormous upside.

Ongoing process or not, just as you set aside time for strategic and annual planning, the leadership cultural framework requires the same commitment. In our opinion, establishing or maintaining a leadership framework provides the foundation for successful and relevant strategic and annual planning.

Moving forward

If you are someone who reads from the back of a book to the front, here is the important "up front part."

"In these tough times, it can't be about popularity or 'pop' fixes; it must be about intentional and consistent leadership and good decisions based upon what we know works, from the experiences of our past."

Michael and Deborah, 2009

When we work with individuals or team clients, we inevitably reach a point where they are ready to move forward. This is the point where leadership challenges are understood and the individual and group work has been done. If you complete the exercises provided, you will understand and appreciate your immediate challenges and you will certainly know what to do next. You will be ready to lead or to lead better.

To recap, we are in a leadership-dependent work world. The twenty-first century offers great challenges and opportunities. Those who embrace the turbulence and volatility and engage their personal and team-based maximum value proposition will not only survive but will prosper and enjoy the ride.

If ever there was a time to activate a practical, applied, and shared leadership approach, this is it. We talked about the leader's role in looking over the horizon and translating to themselves and others what they face. In turn, we talked about the effort that a leader must apply. Twenty percent of her time must be spent in looking to the strategic future. Eighty percent must be spent in leadership conversations with subordinates, peers, and superiors – conversations that are safe and creative; that lead to the expansion of the boundaries of possibility, permission, and forgiveness. These are the conversations that must occur if the maximum value potential of those around us is to be fully utilized. It is this potential that provides the optimal opportunity for us in this century.

We also spent some time talking about vision, values, and behaviour. The boundaries of performance have to be managed with a freedom to manoeuvre for those who agree to be bound by these fundamentals of what we call the Leadership Cultural Framework. It is this fundamental framework that you can develop through the exercises and checklists we have provided.

Along the way, the nuggets provide a whisper from those who have led and continue to lead. Listen carefully to these whisperers. They provide insight into what can work, and if you can connect their thoughts to your current challenges, you can effectively shortcut the learning process and quickly become a more effective influencer. You can share the nuggets with your team or coalition and when you do, don't be surprised if their take is different than yours on the importance and effect that the thoughts and ideas present.

Just as conversations are filtered, we filter our leadership thoughts and ideas through our own experiences. There are no wrong answers, only more insights.

In case you hadn't noticed, this book is about applied leadership – not management process. In order to convey to you the messages we found in our research on applied leadership, we have probably skipped over the value and importance of good management practices, but we know that the best teams are led and inspired by strong leaders who are supported by good management science and processes.

Implicit in our discussion is the fundamental requirement for every leader to accept responsibility. Of all the things discussed, we think, without this fundamental, your leadership potential will be built without a sustainable and consistent foundation. Every interviewee we spoke with indicated in one way or another that this acceptance of responsibility was the key to their followers' trust, their situational credibility, and ultimately their long-term success and reputation.

During our coaching, we consider this to be so important that, when dealing with individual clients, we ask that the client accept responsibility for what has been and what will be. This acceptance is a visible demonstration of a leader's intention and acceptance of his current circumstances and launches him into a higher level of applied leadership.

The significance here is that once this step is taken, you won't want to go back to your pre-applied leadership behaviour. Another significance will be that once other leaders see that you have accepted your leadership responsibility, they will open doors to help you succeed.

Followers seek this kind of leadership. They will want to work with you. To keep them satisfied and growing, you will have to provide clear and understandable vision, a consistent and practised value set, and an agreed and visible behaviour model. It is this agreement on vision, values, and behaviour that forms the basis of your leadership framework and provides the context of permission that encourages maximum-value performance for all.

To keep this balance of leadership influence and followership response in place, there are only three rules that you have to follow:

▶ **Leadership Rule #1:** Commit publicly and privately to make people and the situation better but demand that they do their part, too.

▶ **Leadership Rule #2:** Accept that those whom you commit to help you hold you to Rule #1, because you are intending to hold them to their part. This rule represents the mutually supporting commitment that exists between everyday people who intend on building exceptional teams.

▶ **Leadership Rule #3:** Celebrate your successes in the broadest sense: from the highest mountain with the largest audience. Correct and criticize – or accept criticism – in the narrowest sense: in private.

When we first started talking about applied leadership, it was just talk. Then we decided to live up to our responsibility to do something to help make things and leaders better.

As we were completing our work on this book, we heard John Furlong, Chief Executive Officer, Vancouver Organizing Committee for the 2010 Olympic and Paralympic Winter Games, speak in a video biography.

> "When he arrived in Canada
> more than thirty years ago from Ireland, a customs
> officer offered a warm but specific greeting:
>
> "Welcome to Canada – make us better."

Furlong took those inspired words to heart and within days he was making a contribution, doing what he felt we should all do – giving a little.[7]

The Furlong story reflects what we believe about accepting our leadership responsibility. We accepted our responsibility and wrote this book.

Now it's your turn. And remember,
LEADING MATTERS.

> If you want to improve your ability to lead,
> remember this: make it from the heart!
> *J-P Soublière*

---

7   *www.vancouver2010.com/more-2010-information/about-vanoc/organizing-committee/management-team/john-furlong/john-furlong_882 4Zn.html*

Meet Our Leaders

Gerry Arial

Jean Edouard Boyle

Jim Durrell

Roger Greenberg

Franklin Holtforster

Jacquelin Holzman

France Jacovella

Jan Kaminski

Rosemarie T. Leclair

Rob Lindsay

Jim Orban

Jean-Pierre Soublière

Shannon Tessier

John D. Watts

Gerry Arial

Designer, Creator, President
The Silver Rose

- ▸ Courageous
- ▸ Respectful
- ▸ Energetic
- ▸ Visionary
- ▸ Modest

ON SUCCESSFUL TEAMS:
Successful teams know all that the leader knows and more. They understand the context of things and do not have to be driven to perform. They know what needs to get done, the quality expected, and they simply do it.

ON DEVELOPING PEOPLE:
I believe that every one of my employees has unique properties that allow them to be seen and behave in some high-value way. My role is to set the example and try to stretch myself to understand how I can help them reach just a bit higher each day.

G erry is a world-renowned floral designer and creator and owner of The Silver Rose, an Ottawa landmark floral design company established in 1979. Dramatic elegance is the signature of The Silver Rose, and attention to detail the hallmark.

His arrangements have graced the tables of the famous, the international, and the ordinary citizens of Ottawa. Amongst his clients are: Her Majesty, Queen Elizabeth II, the Prince and Princess of Wales, His Holiness the Pope, several presidents of the United States, and stars of screen and stage, including Bette Davis and Angela Lansbury. Whether it be the Governor General's Performing Arts Awards or the family next door, Gerry's designs are always unique, and his creative approach transforms ordinary space into an extraordinary experience.

A dedicated believer in the growth of others, Gerry has mentored and supported other exceptional floral arrangers with the view that giving back to his business community creates growth and excellence for all.

Gerry Arial and The Silver Rose are titled by Teleflora International as one of the "Top Seven Stellar Florists in the World."

Jean Edouard Boyle, CMM, CD

President & CEO, JEBtek International

- ▶ Vision
- ▶ Honour
- ▶ Drive
- ▶ Action
- ▶ Teamwork

ON LISTENING:
Listening is probably one of the most important characteristics that an individual needs to develop in order to become an effective leader. Listening – *not* delivery, *not* talking – listening.

ON LBWA – LEADERSHIP BY WALKING AROUND:
Get involved. Walk around. Knowing your people and what they are doing is fundamental to influencing them to make positive changes. The good performers will come to you for advice and understanding. Listen to them carefully but make sure that you never let them off the hook. They need continuous challenge!

Jean Boyle brings us forty years of remarkable and decorated experience in executive, command, and senior management portfolios.

He was Chief of the Defence Staff of the Canadian Armed Forces and, prior to that, Assistant Deputy Minister (Personnel), the Department of National Defence. His Command assignments included Commander "1" Canadian Air Division, Germany; Wing Commander "4" Fighter Wing, Germany; Commanding

Officer 433 Fighter Squadron; and Commandant of the Royal Military College of Canada.

He has also proven his mettle in the private sector as chairman of the board, Liska Biometry Inc., chairman of the board of Blue Bear Networks International, managing director, Boeing International Corporation – Europe, and Vice-president International Business Development, the Boeing Company.

Jean is currently president and chief executive officer of JEBtek International. This is an exciting venture providing consulting services to government and industry executives, primarily on complex issues associated with policy, strategy, aerospace markets, and business development within the Canadian and international environment.

Jean resides in Ottawa and is a devoted family man and golfer.

Jim Durrell

President and CEO
Capital Dodge Chrysler Jeep

- ▸ Dynamic
- ▸ Family
- ▸ Community
- ▸ Compelling
- ▸ Direct

ON LEADERSHIP AUTHENTICITY:
Leadership depends on your understanding of your true north, your one true thing that drives everything about you. Without this, you would be a fraud and it would show.

ON RECOGNIZING LEADERSHIP INFLUENCE:
The thing I find most interesting about leadership is that we meet the right people to influence us at the right time to be influenced. The trick might be to recognize that right moment.

James A. Durrell is a former mayor of Ottawa and former president of the Ottawa Senators hockey team. He now works as the owner of a car dealership. Durrell, an insurance executive, was elected to the Ottawa City Council in 1980.

During his time as mayor, Durrell was most closely involved in professional sports; he worked to obtain tax grants for the Ottawa Rough Riders football team. He encouraged a Triple A baseball team to locate in Ottawa and, most notably, he won an NHL franchise for the city.

Soon after that victory, Durrell resigned as mayor of Ottawa to become president of the new hockey club, the Ottawa Senators. He served in this role for a number of years. He bought a car dealership called Capital Dodge Chrysler Jeep and serves in various capacities on a number of boards, including chairman of the Ottawa International Airport and chairman of the Ottawa Congress Centre.

Roger Greenberg

Chairman and CEO, The Minto Group

▶ Family
▶ Customer
▶ Community
▶ Entrepreneur
▶ Honourable

ON FINDING YOUR WAY:
It is key to know where your strengths are. What good is the clear vision if the path you've created to get there is so convoluted that everyone gets lost?

ON COLLABORATION:
In this time of change, silos don't work, reactive approaches are not sustainable, closed organizations cannot survive. If celebrative approaches are not your thing, then this century may not be where you can survive.

Roger Greenberg is the chairman and CEO of The Minto Group, a family-owned real estate business based in Ottawa with operations also in Toronto and South Florida.

Roger was born in Ottawa, where he received his primary and secondary school education. He obtained his Bachelor of Commerce degree at the University of Toronto and then his law degree at Osgoode Hall Law School. He practised real estate law for three years in Toronto before joining Minto on a full-time basis in 1985, when the company expanded its operations to

Toronto. In 1991, Roger moved back to Ottawa to head up the overall operations for the company after the death of his uncle, Irving Greenberg.

Minto is a fully integrated real estate developer, builder, manager, and owner. Since its founding in 1955, Minto has built more than 67,000 homes, including some 12,000 rentals. In 2008, the company built more than 2,200 homes in its three operating locations. It currently manages approximately 14,000 rental homes (owned and third party) and a mixed-use commercial portfolio of approximately two million square feet.

Franklin Holtforster

President and CEO
MHPM Project Managers

▶ Builder
▶ Challenger
▶ Visionary
▶ Trusted
▶ Mentor

ON THE CAPACITY TO LEAD:
A leader is entitled to lead to the extent that people are willing to follow, and the measure of leadership is the extent to which you can influence them to actually follow.

ON RECRUITMENT AND GROWTH:
One of a leader's jobs is to inspire people to recognize and realize their full capability. This is especially important in a resource-constrained environment. It is difficult to find talented people. And it's one thing to get productivity from them, but it's another to unlock their intellectual capability, to get them to undertake more challenging tasks, and to get them to do more than they thought they could.

Franklin Holtforster is president and CEO of MHPM Project Managers Inc. Since founding MHPM in 1989, he has grown the company into fourteen offices in Canada and the United States and established the firm's reputation as a trusted and objective leader of facility projects. He continues to pursue his original objective: to provide clients with the knowledge-able representation required to obtain value on their facilities projects.

His personal experience includes a wide range of projects for both private and public sector clients in Canada and abroad. He recently supported delivery of the $178 million Richmond Olympic Oval that hosted the long-track speed-skating events at the 2010 Vancouver Olympics.

Franklin holds a Bachelor of Applied Science (Civil Engineering), University of Waterloo. He is affiliated with the Association of Professional Engineers of Ontario and the Association of Professional Engineers, Geologists, and Geophysicists of Alberta; he is a Project Management Professional, Project Management Institute, Leadership in Energy and Environmental Design Accredited Professional (LEED AP).

Mr. Holtforster is involved in many activities, including the Owner's Committee, Canadian Design Build Institute; Past Chair, Ottawa Economic Development Corporation; Past Chair, Ottawa Chapter, Professional Engineers Ontario; and War-den – Order of the Iron Ring. He has been honoured as well with the Order of Honour, Professional Engineers Ontario, and the Province of Ontario Volunteer Award.

Franklin is married to Birgitte Alting–Mees, P. Eng. They live in Ottawa with their three sons, aged seven to thirteen.

Jacquelin Holzman

Over Fifty Years of Public Service
and Leadership in Ottawa

▶ Visionary

▶ Inspiring

▶ Tough-minded

▶ Diplomatic

▶ Eloquent

ON VALUES:
Even though there are lots of "pop" psychology and "quick fix"
approaches, if you have a core set of values shared by all, you are
in good shape. We made values very simple and always visible, so
that we were surrounded every day as we walked around.

ON PRIORITIES:
You can't start off with forty-five priorities! Your staff will write
you off right away! Not knowing where you want to go, too many
targets, too many things to do, too much confusion cannot be
good for your team.

J acquelin Holzman has a fifty-year record of exemplary
public service and leadership in Ottawa, particularly in the
academic health science community.

Since 2002, she has chaired the board of directors of the
Ottawa Health Research Institute, the research arm of The
Ottawa Hospital and an affiliated institute of the University of
Ottawa. She served as mayor of Ottawa from 1991 to 1997 and

as city councillor from 1982 to 1991. She also led the Reha-bilitation Institute of Ottawa as president for five years (and served on the board for nineteen years) and chaired the Ottawa Health Science Centre Board during construction of the Ottawa General Hospital, the University of Ottawa Health Sciences Building, and the Royal Ottawa Regional Rehabilitation Centre on Smyth Road.

Ms. Holzman has also made numerous contributions to community organizations such as Algonquin College, the National Capital Commission, the Ottawa Congress Centre, the Boys and Girls Club, Breast Cancer Action, the Kiwanis Club, and the Jewish Social Services Council.

A native Ottawan, she is married to John Rutherford and is the mother of four and the grandmother of four.

France Jacovella

Director General, Multinational/Bilateral Affairs, Environment Canada

- ▸ Courage
- ▸ Diversity
- ▸ Respect
- ▸ Energy
- ▸ Guardianship

ON RECRUITING FOR VALUES:
Hire people based on their values. There will not be complete overlap, rather a sharing and growing together. Sometimes there are deal breakers.

ON LEADERSHIP NETWORKS:
You don't know everything yourself. You need to rely on others to give you advice. Having a network for leaders is important for these kinds of situations and for regular business. You need to bounce ideas off others.

ON KNOWING WHAT YOU DON'T KNOW:
There are things that I don't know that I don't know. You must genuinely listen to others, to discover things that you did not know that you did not know.

France Jacovella is a chemical engineer and holds a Certificate in Management and Administration from the Canadian Institute of Management.

She is currently the Director General, Multilateral and Bilateral Affairs, at Environment Canada and plays a leadership role in the policy and coordination of international environmental activities. She joined the federal public service in June 2001 and has since occupied a variety of positions dealing with the management of chemical substances and wastes, as well as international environmental management. She has extensive operational and management experience in environmental protection, the energy sector, water resource management, and organizational development.

France started her career as a chemical engineer in the oil and gas industry. Prior to joining the federal public service, France held various positions within the region of Ottawa-Carleton related to the management of the waste-water system for that region. She has held positions within the private and public sectors in various fields including operations, regulatory affairs, and policy work.

Jan Kaminski

President, Colonnade Investments

- ▸ Honest
- ▸ Strategic
- ▸ Credible
- ▸ Optimistic
- ▸ Clear
- ▸ Versatile

ON EMPOWERMENT:
One of the things I try to instil is that everyone is the CEO of his/her area. The receptionist is the CEO of reception. The sales rep is the CEO of a territory. The guy doing the packaging and shipping is the CEO of that area. I tell them to make decisions, and if there are things they don't know or don't understand, then it's their job to go and find out — not anybody else's.

ON GROWTH TO LEADERSHIP:
The growing process presents a picture that is almost "messy." This may be a characteristic of the process — leadership is messy . . .

Jan Kaminski has a track record of building successful technology-based companies.

Jan was the president and CEO of Ionalytics Corporation, a start-up company that built analytical instruments used to accelerate the drug discovery and development process. He guided Ionalytics' transition from research to product orientation and led the company through a sale to Thermo Electron.

Jan's previous venture-backed experience was with Fast-Lane Technologies. As president and CEO, Jan built a global sales and support infrastructure that grew to over 1,000 corporate customers. He subsequently led FastLane to a successful sale and integration with Quest Software.

Jan now serves on the board of directors of Manderley Turf Products, Got Corporation, and DNA Genotek. He has also served on the board of Whitehill Technologies and the Commercialization Committee of the Ottawa Hospital Research Institute.

Jan Kaminski holds an MBA from the University of Toronto and a mechanical engineering degree from Queen's University.

Jan resides in Ottawa and is a proud member of a family known for building successful teams and communities.

Rosemarie T. Leclair

President and CEO,
Hydro Ottawa Group of Companies

▶ Customer-focused

▶ Professional

▶ Reflective

▶ Brave

▶ Collaborative

ON HIRING FOR VALUES:
You know, it's not complicated. You hire people for their values and passion. Your challenge is to nurture those things and not let them get lost along the way.

ON BUILDING TRUST:
Trust is built on consistency. People need to know that the way you are going to react to a situation tomorrow is the same as the way you react today. They need to know what to expect.

Rosemarie T. Leclair is president and chief executive officer of the Hydro Ottawa Group of Companies. A seasoned public policy and strategic management professional, Ms. Leclair spent over fifteen years as a senior manager with the City of Ottawa, including a position as Deputy City Manager of Public Works and Services. She has also served as a special advisor to the Province of Ontario.

Ms. Leclair is active in a number of community and industry initiatives, serving as chair of the Business Division for the 2008 United Way/Centraide Ottawa campaign, co-chair of the Employers Council of Champions of the Hire Immigrants Ottawa initiative, and a board member of the Canadian Electricity Association and the Regroupement des gens d'affaires de la Capitale nationale.

Throughout her career, Ms. Leclair has been a champion for numerous sustainability initiatives, including Project Porchlight and Earth Hour. In 2007, Ms. Leclair was named one of Canada's Top 100 Most Powerful Women by the Women's Executive Network.

She holds a degree in Public Administration and a Bachelor of Laws from the University of Ottawa and became a member of the Law Society of Upper Canada in 1985.

Rob Lindsay

CPGA Head Professional
Hylands Golf & Country Club

▸ Compassionate

▸ Fair

▸ Listens

▸ Loyal

▸ Customer-driven

ON LEADERSHIP INFLUENCE:
Leadership is a heavy burden — to be that influential. I want to be sure my team leaders understand the need to lead prudently and carefully.

ON BUILDING CAPACITY FROM POTENTIAL:
Employees with real potential often react best when the leader just poses the problem, letting the solutions flow from the employees' capacity and experience. Maybe there are cleaner, less messy ways to get from here to there, but none that build real teamwork as well.

Rob started in the golf business in 1991 at the Ottawa Hunt Club as an assistant professional. In 2001, Rob accepted the position of head professional at Hylands Golf Club in Ottawa and has enjoyed the people and challenges of developing a business ever since.

Rob is a member of the advisory staff for the Titleist golf

company and in 2008 won the Club Professional of the Year for the Ottawa Valley Zone of the PGA.

Rob and his wife, Claudine, have two daughters, Jessy and Maya.

Jim Orban

Publisher (former)
The Ottawa Citizen

▶ Complex

▶ Intuitive

▶ Observant

▶ Brave

▶ Private

ON LEADING IN ALL DIRECTIONS:
Part of a leader's job is to make sure he is leading outside in, top down, and bottom up.

ON LEADING IN THIS CENTURY:
Many industries are just now coming to grips with the fact that their leadership is sitting in the last century, while the employees are working in this century.

ON KNOWING WHEN TO INFLUENCE:
A leader must know when to throw himself in front of the bullets and take one for the team and when to back off. Sometimes you cannot stop things from happening and you cannot always influence what others think or do.

A fter starting his newspaper career in 1972 at the Ottawa Journal, Jim worked at the Ottawa Citizen (1975) and the Edmonton Journal (1991) before returning to the Citizen in 1994. In 2003, he was appointed to the position of publisher, responsible for all aspects of producing the Citizen.

In recognition of Jim's professional and community leadership, he has received numerous awards, including the Civic Entrepreneur of the Year Award (2002) and the Trudeau Medal from the University of Ottawa (2004). He was the first recipient of the "Just One Person" award in 2006, which launched a scholarship at the University of Ottawa exclusively for youth-in-care.

Jim holds a Master of Business Administration degree from the University of Ottawa. In 2002, the Telfer School of Management at the University of Ottawa established the $50,000 "James E. Orban Scholarship" to award annual bursaries to students demonstrating leadership and academic excellence.

For over thirty years, Jim has been involved in many community and newspaper organizations and is currently active in thirteen community advisory/foundation boards. He also serves on the Canadian Newspaper Association board of directors.

Jean–Pierre Soublière

President, Anderson Soublière Inc.

- ▶ Visionary
- ▶ Character first
- ▶ Innovator
- ▶ Creative
- ▶ Value
- ▶ Vision

ON LEADING CHANGE:
We may be just at the beginning of the change, even though we feel we are further into it than that.

ON RECRUITING FOR LEADERSHIP:
When we hire, we look first at attributes, character, and value, then at community involvement, then at skills and the "tech" things. Am I being clear about where our priorities are?

ON VALUE-BASED PRIORITIES:
The real issue is always "doing the right thing." It may not even be important to do it really well, but just to do it! I think that there are many "right things" that just don't get done because we get sidetracked with all the other stuff. Sometimes it's really hard to figure out what the "right thing" to do is, but it's funny that in our hearts, we always know what we shouldn't do!

J ean–Pierre Soublière is the president of Anderson Soublière Inc., an executive-focused consulting corporation. He was also the president and COO of Alis Technologies and president, Systemhouse Canada and International.

J-P has served his community well and in many ways for numerous corporations, councils, boards, associations, universities, and campaigns. Currently, he is a member of several councils and boards, including the University of Ottawa, the Harmony Foundation (chair), the May Court Hospice, Accreditation Canada, the advisory board of Talent Map Inc., the OLG, Toro TV (chair), the E-Health Council of the Champlain Local Health Integration Network (chair), and the Audit Committee of Public Works Government Services Canada.

He was named Business Person of the Year (1995) by the Ottawa–Carleton Board of Trade. He was also awarded the 1996 Prix d'Excellence by the Regroupement des gens d'affaires, the 1997 Trudeau Medal by the University of Ottawa, the President's Award as a volunteer for United Way in Ottawa in 1996, the Queen's Golden Jubilee Medal (2002), the Order of Ottawa for Economic Development (2004), and the 2006 Award of Distinction, United Way Canada.

J-P is a graduate of the University of Ottawa (BCom 1967), the University of British Columbia (MBA 1971), and the Institute of Corporate Directors (2008).

He is a member of the Rideau Club, the RGA, and the Hunt Golf and Country Club; but mostly he is the proud husband of Cathie. Together, their key achievement consists of four married children, and grandchildren.

Shannon Tessier

B.Sc. (honours), Researcher, Volunteer

- ▶ Researcher
- ▶ Energetic
- ▶ Wise
- ▶ Committed
- ▶ Respectful

ON THE BURDEN OF LEADERSHIP:
Leadership brings its burdens. You have to take the time to know yourself, your boundaries, limits, strengths, and, of course, your areas for more development.

ON TEAMS:
Give your team members some room to grow, to problem-solve on their own; trust them. Simply put, your leadership job is really to create the right conditions for others to grow.

Shannon attended Carleton University for her Bachelor of Science degree in Biology with highest honours in 2007 and started her Master's in molecular biology and biochemistry in September of 2008. Shannon's most significant contribution to research and development is her work on muscle atrophy and hypertrophy. She is a primary researcher in understanding the molecular mechanisms that will help unravel medical disorders such as hypertrophic cardiomyopathy. This initiative and her research are supported by the National Sciences and Engineering Research Council of Canada. Shannon is a recipient of the Alexander Graham Bell Canada Graduate Scholarship award.

Shannon also works as a teaching assistant at Carleton University and has worked as a learning strategy assistant for Carleton University students with disabilities. In five years' time, she would like to be a lead researcher, working to deliver outstanding results.

Shannon is the president of the Charity of Hope to Assist Needy Children Everywhere (CHANCE), which she founded with her mother, Lorna. She is involved in many other community-based organizations, including the Let's Talk Science program and CTV's Youth Advisory Board. In appreciation for Shannon's community involvement, the National Capital Region YMCA–YWCA recognized Shannon as a Young Woman of Distinction on June 1, 2009.

John D. Watts

President (former)
General Dynamics

▶ Gentleman

▶ Intuitive

▶ Principled

▶ Entrepreneur

▶ Collaborator

ON WORKING TOWARD THE SAME GOAL:
There is nothing more difficult than when you've got people
rowing a boat in different directions. You get there eventually
but it takes you a lot longer. You need to create the vision for
employees. You have to ensure that they know what it means
for them. Then you will row in the same direction and get there
faster.

ON BRICKS AND MORTAR:
At the end of the day you can tear the building down, because
it is just bricks and mortar. And you can take away all the
equipment. But it is the people that make the whole thing work.
It's compassion and understanding for the people that are the key
to leadership.

Born September 4, 1946, in Rugby, England, Mr. Watts
served a commercial apprenticeship with GEC and subsequently joined Ford Motor Company, where he held several
financial positions before immigrating to Canada in 1975.

Mr. Watts joined Computing Devices Canada Ltd. in 1976 and held successive positions within the financial organization, becoming chief financial officer (CFO) in 1982. He was appointed senior vice-president in 1994. In this capacity, he was responsible for the general management of the Ottawa operations; he had specific responsibility for three of the company's major business units, including research and development, marketing, and program management, as well as total responsibility for the manufacturing operation that supports both Canadian facilities.

Mr. Watts holds a CMA and ACIS designation and is on the board of directors of General Dynamics Canada Ltd. He is an active board member of the Canadian Association of Defence & Security Industries (CADSI), the Conference of Defence Associations (CDA) Institute, and the Canadian NATO Industrial Advisory Group (CNIAG).

Mr. Watts is married with three children.

Appendices

APPENDIX A
Leadership Cultural Framework Checklist

Your goal is to embrace each of the Leadership Cultural Framework Steps to bring your applied leadership vision to life. These steps establish where you are and where you are going.

Step 1. **Conceptualize** your applied leadership vision

Step 2. **Design** your framework

Step 3. **Build** your framework

Step 4. **Activate and deploy** your framework

Step 5. **Monitor and improve** your framework and vision

Step 1. Conceptualize your applied leadership vision

√	TASKS
	Complete the KWYK/KWYDK (Know What You Know/Know What You Don't Know) Knowledge Grid Tool (Section 3)
	▸ Have I explored the ten key leadership competencies?
	1. Strategic thinking
	2. Self-confidence
	3. Ethics and integrity
	4. Creativity and innovation
	5. Flexibility and adaptability
	6. Ability to inspire vision
	7. Communication and information
	8. Building relationships
	9. Teamwork
	10. Management and empowerment
	▸ Do I recognize what I know and what I don't know?
	▸ Do I recognize what my team knows and doesn't know?
	Complete the Leadership Self-Assessment Tool (Section 3)
	▸ Have I completed the six self-assessments?
	1. Self-Knowledge and Authenticity
	2. Leadership Value Proposition
	3. Vision and Values
	4. Coaching Others and Collaboration
	5. Building Trust
	6. Credibility and Authority
	▸ Have I identified my leadership strengths and the opportunities for my development?
	Do a SWOT (Strengths/Weaknesses/Opportunities/Threats) of your self-knowledge (below)
	What do you conclude from this?
	Have I summarized my integrated and prioritized leadership development opportunities?
	Environment: Have I identified my short-, medium-, and long-term challenges? Can I translate these challenges to others: superiors, peers, and subordinates?

	Action/Objective/Goal: From the above, what are the five key actions, objectives, and goals that will require you and your team's attention due to your assessment of the rationale and risks associated with each?
	Urgency: Do I understand the urgency of the challenges I face? Am I able to transmit that urgency to others in an honest and clear way?
	Believers: Have I identified those who believe in me? Will they understand my vision and their role in helping me to accomplish it?
	Non-Believers: What about the non-believers?
	Leadership Vision: Can I see clearly the outcome? Have I written it down? Do I know what success looks like?
	Communication: Do I understand my communications strengths and the potential mechanisms to deliver my messages?

SWOT of total self-knowledge

SWOT stands for Strengths, Weaknesses, Opportunities, and Threats. This is an easy-to-use and widely accepted method to facilitate brainstorming new outputs and ideas from existing information and situations. Here's how it works:

1. **Strengths:** Look back at your notes from each of the six self-assessments. Identify the top strengths for each assessment. Record them in the SWOT chart below.

2. **Weaknesses:** Do the same as above.

3. **Opportunities:** This step requires you to think about possible positive ideas, goals, objectives, or actions that flow naturally from your strengths and weaknesses. For example, if you identified a weakness in communicating with your team, there is an opportunity to improve. What might that be? It could be to plan regular opportunities to share information, to meet more regularly, to be better prepared, and so on.

4. **Threats:** Threats can be derived from internal or external sources. Internal threats come from the sum of your strengths, opportunities, and weaknesses. If you know you have a communication problem and do nothing, you are accepting that you have a possible threat related to poor communication. External threats can include issues such as not having a corporate plan; or team members, peers, or superiors not aligned with your framework.

SWOT CHART

STRENGTHS	WEAKNESSES

OPPORTUNITIES	THREATS

What do you conclude from this?

	MY PRIORITIZED LEADERSHIP DEVELOPMENT OPPORTUNITIES
1	
2	
3	
4	
5	
6	
7	
8	
9	
10	

ENVIRONMENT – Have I identified my short-, medium-, and long-term challenges? Can I translate these challenges to others – superiors, peers, and subordinates?

	SHORT RANGE – LEADERSHIP ACTIONS I NEED TO TAKE IN THE NEXT NINETY DAYS	WHY
1		
2		
3		

	MEDIUM RANGE – TACTICAL LEADERSHIP OBJECTIVES TO CONSIDER IN THE NEXT YEAR	WHY
1		
2		
3		

	LONG RANGE – STRATEGIC LEADERSHIP GOALS TO CONSIDER IN THE NEXT TWO YEARS	WHY – RATIONALE AND RISKS/CONSEQUENCES
1		
2		
3		

From the above, what are the five key actions, objectives, and goals that will require you and your team's attention due to your assessment of the rationale and risks associated with each?

	ACTION/OBJECTIVE/GOAL
1	
2	
3	
4	
5	

URGENCY — Do I understand the urgency of the challenges I face? Am I able to transmit that urgency to others in an honest and clear way?

Having brought yourself this far — that is, you have completed a leadership inventory, you have identified strengths, weaknesses, opportunities, and threats that affect you and your team, and you have identified the priority items that you believe require resolution or action — it is time to pause and focus on the real urgency to move forward. Your sense of urgency must be real. Others will be influenced to either follow and adapt or not, based upon your clear identification and transmission of the urgency and the consequences (positive and negative).

Take a deep breath. Think it through again. Does it need to be done?

Fine, let's do it.

BELIEVERS — Have I identified those who believe in me? Will they understand what I see and their role in helping me to accomplish it?

From across the spectrum of your organizational relationship — subordinates, peers, and superiors — there will be those who you already know are your believers. Identify them and their potential contribution.

	MY BELIEVERS	AREA OF CONTRIBUTION
1		
2		
3		
4		
5		
6		
7		
8		
9		
10		

You also need to develop a list of non-believers. These would be anyone from your internal subordinates, peers, and superiors to your stakeholders. This is not a list of those you wish to co-opt but rather a list of those who will critique and challenge, positively or negatively. They will force you to examine every aspect of your vision. You need them, although they might never agree with you.

	MY NON-BELIEVERS	AREA OF CONTRADICTION
1		
2		
3		
4		
5		
6		
7		
8		
9		
10		

LEADERSHIP VISION – Can I see clearly the outcome? Have I written it down? Do I know what success looks like?

At this point you have analyzed, tabulated, and prioritized the merits of where you are planning to go, when, and to some degree how you will get there. Now you need to succinctly write down your intention(s). To make it simple, divide it into three parts. Start with the longer-range vision. Add the supporting steps (including what, who, when, how, etc.) to get there. It might look like this:

MY LEADERSHIP VISION SAMPLE:

GOAL:	To build an organizational leadership development program based upon my SWOT assessment of me and my team.
WHEN:	Deployment by 2012
WHO:	HR and Corporate Services
WHAT:	The program will:
	▶ Result in leadership coaching tools for individuals and groups
	▶ Be affordable to develop and effective
	▶ Fit with the corporate culture and plan
	▶ Be easily implemented with existing resources
	▶ Be multicultural and transportable to all corporate divisions
HOW:	By:
	▶ Subcontracting development and/or delivery, or
	▶ Internal development and support
SUCCESS:	I will know we have been successful when:
	▶ Delivery by 2012
	▶ Corporate culture accepts leadership development is a critical success factor for organizational success
	▶ When turnover is reduced and employee engagement and performance increase over time

COMMUNICATION – Do I understand my communications strengths and the potential mechanisms to deliver my messages?

There are three basic mechanisms to communicate through:

▶ Personal
▶ Documentation
▶ Combination of personal and documentation approaches

Some combination of the above with the following possible delivery vehicles:

► Face-to-face
► One-on-one
► Electronic

These can be delivered to:

► Team(s)
► Coalition(s)
► Supervisor(s)
► Peer(s)
► Stakeholder(s)

We are not trying to be comprehensive here – we are only providing some samples of the delivery mechanisms you might consider. Use what works for you. The medium that you are most comfortable with will likely be the one to get your message across – initially, at least – the most clearly.

You will also need to consider the transmission differences between initial and subsequent messaging. Don't forget to establish a communication and information management approach (including configuration control, delivery vehicles, venues, etc.).

Step 2. Design your framework

√	TASKS
	► Anchor your strategic plan.
	► Walk through your leadership vision.
	► Consolidate your vision.

► **Anchor your strategic plan.** Secure an agreement on the future from your superior(s). Make sure you are on the same page with them with respect to goals, priorities, resources, timing, and urgency.

► **Walk through your leadership vision.**

With peers – Take the leadership vision for the future developed in concept and modified with your superior(s) and present it to your entire peer group. Tap into the expertise and talent of those around you to refine it. Make sure the things you now are planning are appropriate to the peer group (e.g., no unnecessary overlaps). You are actually getting their support as well as getting their advice. Do they clearly understand and endorse your view of your team's future state, including strategic challenges and resource factors (time, money, talent)?

With subordinates – Using the leadership vision as a base, consult your subordinates and allow them to brainstorm with you to ensure that the future goals, priorities, and general effort take advantage of team strengths, while minimizing the risks of team weaknesses. Do they convey to you their assessment of the consequences of the vision? Are you listening?

With stakeholders – Identify those key stakeholders who will be affected by your goals, priorities, timing, and urgency. Work with them to identify potential roadblocks, success factors, and dis-satisfiers. Can you accommodate the needs of stakeholders in your final plan?

With non-believers – Prove your modified leadership vision with those most likely to critique or be critical. Do not defend! Listen with an open mind. Ask questions. Revisit consequences and risks. This is your last chance to modify your design before building it into a leadership framework.

▶ **Consolidate your vision.** Redraft, as required, the concept, taking into account the adjustments from the advice that you have received and accepted.

Step 3. Build your framework

The integration of all the elements into a homogeneous framework is your objective. You can do this for yourself or with your team by:

▶ Translating the future state and what success will look like based upon your consolidated leadership vision

▶ Confirming the organizational and work context. Have you forgotten anything?

▶ Establishing team and individual strengths and areas for development as a team and for individuals

▶ Discussing and establishing behavioural norms (this is a team activity; or if this is for yourself only, consult your coalition or believer group)

▶ Setting the limits for permission and forgiveness (to be discussed privately with each of your direct reports)

▶ Establishing a consistent personal or team (corporate and cascading) value set

▶ Developing mechanisms for living by Leadership Rules #1, #2, and #3

▶ Establishing a personal or team monitoring and measurement process

▶ Building mechanisms for personal or team leadership and management performance assessments

▶ Creating a clear, written, and accessible record of your critical outcomes: vision, values, and behaviours

▶ Accepting responsibility for your own leadership performance. For teams, by delegating to each team member a sensible leadership development plan that will meet both the organization's and the individual's needs (e.g., coaching, training, assignment, formal education, mentoring, etc.).

Step 4. Activate and deploy your framework

Activation means you (and everyone on your team) are on the same leadership cultural page at the same time and able to answer the following questions:

▶ What is included and does it work?

▶ How is it integrated into the management processes and leadership style?

- ▶ Does it exist at all levels? If not, why not?
- ▶ How do you talk about it and use it?
- ▶ Is it safe to talk about it?
- ▶ Who is the keeper?
- ▶ Who is the inspirational source?
- ▶ How is it kept alive? Is there a feedback loop?
- ▶ How is it measured?
- ▶ How will you know if you are successful?

The next step is deployment. The Leadership Cultural Framework becomes your foundation. It is the key reference point – for recruitment, selection, retention, performance, promotion, and succession.

Step 5. Monitor and improve your framework and vision

Monitoring and improvement can be as simple as regularly scheduled leadership conversations where the topic is the framework, how it is being utilized, and whether it is still relevant or in need of rethinking. This leadership conversation could be internal or assisted by external advisors – it doesn't matter how you get this done but the conversation, in itself, is essential.

To determine the effectiveness of your framework across each of the areas (recruitment, selection, retention, performance, promotion, and succession) will be a challenge. Employee surveys, customer satisfaction surveys, grievances, and employee engagement reviews are all legitimate pointers. Make no mistake – this is about people, feelings, inspiration, motivation, and connectivity. The only way that is close to getting you the true picture will be to continually conduct intentional conversations at all levels concerning the framework, its legitimacy, and the commitment to it by everyone.

This is an ongoing process that requires discipline and focus but has an enormous upside.

Ongoing process or not, just as you set aside time for strategic and annual planning, the leadership cultural framework requires the same commitment. In our opinion, establishing or maintaining a leadership framework provides the foundation for successful and relevant strategic and annual planning.

APPENDIX B
Leadership in Action —
The Kaminski List

Have I been . . . ?

1. Consistent, secure, and confident in myself, my beliefs, and my actions?

2. Good at making big problems small?

3. Always giving an individual the benefit of the doubt?

4. Overreacting to good news and under-reacting to bad news?

5. Not asking anyone to do something I wouldn't do myself?

6. Not doing something that someone else should be doing?

7. Putting my honour, integrity, and reputation above my personal gain?

8. Knowing my strengths and limitations?

9. Aware that I can't do it all myself?

10. Relying on others' strengths?

11. Coaching others' limitations?

12. Acknowledging that people make mistakes as part of the learning and development process?

13. Testing and challenging others, myself, and the organization?

14. Saying, "I made a mistake"?

15. Saying things like: "What do you think?"

16. Critical of systems, processes, and the work environment before I am critical of the people involved?

17. Trying to put myself in the other person's shoes?

18. Always learning how to lead?

19. Jumping to conclusions?

20. Putting the team ahead of the individual?

21. Aware of how and when to follow?

22. Acknowledging the need for other formal and informal leaders in order to have a successful team?

23. Focusing on the positives and constructively analyzing the negatives?

24. Results-oriented but knowing I can't manage results, only objectives and actions?

25. Sensitive to change?

26. Visible and making myself that way?

27. Seeing the team and individuals succeed?

28. Careful not to take business issues personally?

29. Taking leadership personally?

30. . . . LEADING?

APPENDIX C
Don't Stand There Waiting

Leadership is action, not a position

Manage Things *and* People

MANAGEMENT	LEADERSHIP
Processes	People
Facts	Feelings
Head	Heart
Position power	Persuasion power
Control	Commitment
Problem-solving	Possibility thinking
Reactive	Proactive
Doing things right	Doing the right things
Rules	Values
Goals	Vision
Light fire under	Stoke fire within
Written communication	Verbal communication
Standardization	Innovation

Use phrases like:

How can I help you?

What do you think about . . . ?

Got any ideas?

How can we get this done?

In your experience, what works best?

What problems are we facing?

Do you have enough budget/ time/help/knowledge?

Well done!

Thank you; a great effort!

Let's talk about priorities.

Let me tell you about where we are going.

Let's talk about how things are going so far.

What are we learning?

Let's try again.

No problem—we can do it!

SUCCESSFUL LEADERS

▶ Are confident — they have an inner confidence. They don't say they are great. They know their job and where they are going. They exhibit confidence.

▶ Do not need to know all the answers. They are leading a team of people and they create an environment where people participate actively and creatively in problem solving.

▶ Do not need, and they legitimately and actively share, the glory. They acknowledge people who contribute. They do not hog the glory. They develop an environment where people can say what they think — good — bad — right — wrong.

▶ Hold people accountable but do not embarrass or humiliate people who make errors or have a bad idea

▶ Give verbal and written acknowledgement of effort. They reward effort within their bounds — monetary, perks, etc.

▶ Are organized. Everyone knows their role and tasks. These are discussed and agreed to.

▶ Are very good listeners — to new ideas

▶ Are flexible. If a plan is wrong or not working, they are not worried about adjusting midstream. They are not worried about their own ego.

▶ Provide support — moral, technical, and labour — to people to help them get their tasks done

BAD LEADERS:

▶ Are the opposite of above

▶ Are confident to the point where they take credit for things that go right but blame or are abusive when things go wrong

▶ Do not accept anything that does not agree with their plan. Solutions have to be their solutions.

▶ Don't listen or provide an environment to solicit ideas. They want toadies.

▶ Are afraid of confident people around them and make sure they don't have them, because they are afraid of losing their own position

▶ Do not share the total plan. They "divvy" out pieces of it to secure their own future.

▶ Do not acknowledge people's contributions but take credit

▶ Say, "do what I say"

Dave Dickson

APPENDIX D

Leadership Assessment Tools

H ere are some helpful leadership assessment tools you might encounter. These are all commercially available, usually through career counsellors or others who have completed some level of certification in their use.

Personality Inventories

FIRO–B: Published by Consulting Psychologists Press, *www.cpp. com/products/firo-b/index.asp*, the FIRO–B helps people understand how their needs for inclusion, control, and affection shape their interactions with others.

Myers–Briggs Type Indicator: Published by Consulting Psychologists Press, *www.cpp.com/products/mbti/index.asp*, the MBTI is a widely used instrument for identifying individual strengths and helping people become more self-aware and more effective with others.

Multi–Rater and 360° Assessments

The 360° feedback method systematically collects opinions about someone's performance from a wide range of co-workers: peers, the boss, the boss's peers, and any direct reports. It can be expensive for an organization to conduct, but an employee gets to see a wide range of perceptions of his or her work, which is usually more helpful than just self-perception or a supervisor's view.

Benchmarks, Prospector, and *360 by Design* are products developed by the Center for Creative Leadership and administered by trainers they certify. *www.ccl.org/leadership/assessments/assessment360.aspx*

Self-Assessments

Self-assessments are scored and interpreted by the individual completing the assessment. They can provide immediate insight into leadership characteristics, developmental assignments, and preferred learning styles.

Learning Tactics Inventory, Job Challenge Profile, Campbell Leadership Descriptor, and *Campbell Interest and Skill Survey (CISS)* are products sold by the Center for Creative Leadership.

www.ccl.org/leadership/assessments/SelfAssessments-Overview.aspx?pageId=83

About the Authors

Deborah and Michael met by chance in 2007, and their mutual interest in exploring the topic of leadership was the catalyst that led to their partnership and this work. Michael and Deborah have collaborated on and delivered their inspirational and common-sense approach to leadership for teams and individuals throughout the public and private sectors in the Ottawa region. The people they meet and coach are a constant inspiration to them.

Michael Morin

Michael (Mike) Morin is a Senior Leadership and Career Transition Coach at KWA Partners (Ottawa) Limited. A former Canadian Forces senior officer and base commander, he served over thirty-two years in the air force in Canada and abroad.

During his military career, he was appointed to the Order of Military Merit (at the rank of officer) and has been awarded the NATO Service Medal (with Bar), the Queen's Jubilee Medal, and the Canadian Service Medal (with two clasps).

For his work in promoting military training and education for Hungarian forces in Canada, in 1995 he was awarded a "Title of Distinction" for Home Defence (First Class) by the Government of the Republic of Hungary.

Michael is a graduate of the Canadian Forces Staff College.

Michael and his wife, Cheryl, live in Ottawa. They are the proud parents of three great children and their wonderful partners and are the very proud grandparents of six.

Deborah Dickson

Deborah Dickson is a Senior Leadership Associate at KWA Partners (Ottawa) Limited and an independent management consultant. Throughout her distinguished career she has used her multidisciplined background in leadership and organizational development, information technology, and strategic planning in a wide range of industrial and crown corporations.

Deborah graduated in Business Administration, Information Technology, from Conestoga College and attended Wilfrid Laurier University.

Along with her husband, Dave, Deborah lives in Almonte, Ontario. They have four boys, all with unique personalities and pursuing their dreams, careers, and athletic passions; wonderful daughters-in-law; and five fabulous grandchildren.

TO ORDER MORE COPIES:

GENERAL STORE PUBLISHING HOUSE
499 O'Brien Road, Box 415, Renfrew, Ontario, Canada K7V 4A6
Tel 1.800.465.6072 • Fax 1.613.432.7184
www.gsph.com